Tom W. Johnson

16 September 1972

£6

BUSES ANNUAL

BUSES ANNUAL 1973

Edited by
GAVIN BOOTH

LONDON
IAN ALLAN

First published 1972

SBN 7110 0373 4

Published by Ian Allan Ltd., Shepperton,
Surrey, and printed in the United Kingdom
by A. Wheaton & Co., Exeter

Contents

Preceding pages: A Huddersfield Daimler CVG6-30
climbs high from Halifax to its home town on the
joint service between these two towns.

Introduction

This year's *Buses Annual* has two main themes. One is nostalgia. Just like the man who condemned sex and violence on television with the argument that he could get enough of these at home, we avoid too many reminders of service cuts, strikes and fare rises; the weekly and monthly trade papers keep us informed of the often grim realities of present-day bus and coach operation. The Glasgow Leyland Titan PD3 and the nearby newspaper bill on the front cover are further reminders.

Instead, we are caught in the current wave of unashamed nostalgia, to help while away those long winter evenings. There is nostalgia from Charles Klapper, remembering the early days in London, from John Parke on prewar Cornwall, from Gortonian on Thornycrofts in the Tame Valley, from Alan Townsin on London's STL class and from J. E. Dunabin on Herefordshire. Other articles are more topical, moving about the Scottish Highlands and North Staffordshire.

Our other main theme is Europe. As Britain moves closer to the continent we look at Europe's bus builders—the opposition—and Robert E. Jowitt takes a characteristic look at double-deckers in several countries.

Once again we have tried to cover a wide range of areas and interests, a difficult task in 132 pages. Once again we hope you find the *Annual* enjoyable.

Gavin Booth
Edinburgh

Thornycrofts in the Tame Valley

GORTONIAN follows their fortunes with SHMD

The pioneer LC vehicle, 118, in normal service passing through Ashton whilst en route to Glossop.

As I have remarked before one of the saddest features of present day life is the slow but steady disappearance of many of the smaller undertakings which have so intrigued enthusiasts in the past. Most of these possessed a very mixed bag of automotive assets, which only enhanced their charm, but one or two combined interesting routes with a highly standardised but fascinating fleet, and in the case with which I propose to deal here this standardisation principle covered almost the entire heavy duty passenger vehicle history of a manufacturer whose activities are now only seldom referred to in passenger transport literature, namely the Basingstoke based firm of Thornycroft, that took up the construction of this type of chassis in about 1923.

The operator was none other than the erstwhile Stalybridge, Hyde, Mossley and Dukinfield Joint Tramways and Electricity Board and right from the very start of our

triangular acquaintance it was a case of "love at first sight", at least so far as I was concerned.

We met one wet Saturday night in Stockport about 1929, when I noticed among a large number of red buses and trams a single green tramcar that suddenly appeared out of nowhere into the middle of Mersey Square. It had a character all of its own and I pleaded with my parents for a ride but they were intent on boarding our homeward bound Tilling-Stevens and my urgent requests were very firmly denied.

The same thing happened again about a year later, when we made a first excursion

7

to Mossley, but then came occasion number three when we went back again on another Saturday afternoon, being en route *en famille* for Millbrook and on leaving Mossley Station made a beeline for another green tramcar (or Green Linnet in local parlance) which was obligingly parked right outside the booking office door.

The driver alas said we wanted not a tramcar but a bus, a conveyance that would be along shortly and so in a mood of almost despair I watched the tram take off and grind away down the sloping street until it passed out of sight when my attention was taken by the arrival of the aforementioned vehicle, and what a machine that was.

It was tall, short, thin and so archaic in general appearance than the monarch after whom the model was named might well have ridden upon it for this was a Thornycroft Boadicea with a Northern Counties body and here was standardisation in tandem for the undertaking was to remain faithful to both manufacturers for as long as it was able to do so.

The very first Joint Board buses were number 71 to 74 inclusive, cost £1,120 each complete and entered service on May 30, 1925 between Hyde Market Place and Woolley Bridge on the edge of Glossop, under powers obtained in July 1923. This innovation was designed to counter a North Western Road Car excursion into SHMD territory over the same route, and resulted in the withdrawal of the Hyde to Mottram tramway service although some track out of Hyde had to be left in working order to allow access to the depot there.

These new buses had the AB 4 four cylinder petrol engine, which had overhead inlet and side exhaust valves, a cone clutch, and a four forward speed crash gear box. On to the chassis went a Northern Counties 26-seat body and this had both front and rear doorways. Initially a two-man crew was carried .

Three months later another four built to the same design appeared and they pioneered an Ashton to Mossley and Haddens route which enable the single-deck tramcars working on the Mossley to Haddens section to be almost eliminated. Single-deck operation was required due to the steep gradient from Mossley Station to the unfortunately named "Brookbottom" which is perched precipitously high above the station.

The last of these vehicles another batch of four numbers 79 to 82 came into use in December 1925 and now the Board had 12 buses but not for long.

January 1926 saw the arrival of a demonstrator registration number HO 6437 which was quickly nicknamed the "Red Bus" due to its colour. A 20-seater of type A1 it possessed something dear to local hearts namely Northern Counties carpentry with only a single front door. It must though have been a successful experiment for it was purchased in April 1926 and given the fleet number 91 when it was repainted to become identical to numbers 83 to 90 that had been obtained in the meantime. All nine of these buses were worked right from the start on the one-man principle and this was extended to the rest of the fleet after the ending of the General Strike of May 1926.

The Board's main interests in 1927/8 was to develop its bus activities and thus restrict competition, a policy which required further vehicles and so a large batch of 26-seat machines came into use between June 1927 and April 1928, commencing with number 92 and running up to number 109.

With them came a reversion to the two-door layout, but although their UB type chassis still had normal control the long bonnets concealed a new and rather larger all side valve engine than that previously employed, in this case the MB 4. The braking system also differed from what had gone before. Retardation was dependent on the strength of the driver as no servos were incorporated but presumably a foot brake which acted on both the transmission and the front wheels together with a hand brake acting on the rear wheels sufficed for all practical purposes.

The six buses delivered in the December 1927/January 1928 period were used to replace the Ashton to Hyde via Dukinfield tramway service that was withdrawn on

8

January 11, 1928—yet another single-deck service but in this instance it was low railway bridges and not steep gradients that were the restricting factors.

Only two single-deck tramway services now remained, both starting in Ashton Old Square and running to Acres Lane via Tame Valley or the Albion Hotel. Again low bridges were responsible for the type of car used. They lasted until August 28, 1928 when an agreement with Ashton Corporation as to the use of the necessary tracks in that borough expired and then these larger Thornycrofts took over.

In later years a great deal of very necessary work was put in hand by the highway authorities and after the tramway tracks had been removed and road surfaces lowered double-deck motor buses could be employed instead of the single deckers on these heavily trafficked local routes, but double-deckers were not in

Bus 72, one of the original Boadicea models of 1925. Note how a separate driver's cab was provided despite the lack of space resulting from the normal control layout.

mind when the next series of Thornycrofts came into stock although they were much more suitable for this type of work.

They were four in number with the fleet identities 110 to 113 inclusive, and at £1,250 each were some £80 dearer than their predecessors, but extra cash had produced extra bus and so their UBX chassis although retaining the MB 4 petrol engine had forward control thus allowing the Northern Counties body to have both two doors and 32 seats. Because of their "size" and operating sphere conductors were carried.

New in the December 1928/January 1929 period they were followed in May 1929 by

9

Thornycroft frontage. 112, one of the first four forward control models, poses in the snow prior to entering service in January 1929.

DEPOT ONLY

THORNYCROFT
LG·137

another four numbered consecutively up to 117.

After the UBX came the LC which was different only in the gear change operating mechanism layout, and no less than 24 of these machines came into stock as numbers 118 to 141 between December 1929 and May 1930. Some went to replace further tramcars, some to open new bus routes, and some to make possible the end of the first generation of Joint Board buses as fifteen of their older sisters were withdrawn from passenger work in the same period, but successful though the LC was, its life was not to be over long as all were taken out of use in their turn between 1939 and 1940 but by then not all remained in their original condition.

The MB 4 petrol engine as the designation implies had four cylinders and actually produced 60 bhp at 1800 rpm which was by no means excessive for what was then a full-sized single-decker destined for work on a number of steeply-graded routes, so in 1933 or 1934 six came to acquire the Thornycroft CIND4 4¾in bore compression ignition engine which put out 90 bhp at the same crank shaft speed. The vehicles involved were numbers 122, 123, 124, 125, 134 and 135.

As was only to be expected, however, the extra torque quite upset the half shafts which snapped off at alarmingly low mileages until someone had the idea of calling in Vickers who cooked up a high quality steel, and so ended that annoyance.

Along with the diesel engine came exhausters which certainly improved vacuum availability and heavier flywheels which did likewise in so far as "tickover" was concerned, but here there was an unwanted side effect for gear changing was rendered much more difficult until the revised technique of waiting until the revs had died down had been mastered.

By and large this first Basingstoke essay into oil fuel operation following experiments with Mercedes, Gardner and Dorman-powered goods vehicles was quite successful, but we have digressed so let us return to the main stream of fleet progress.

No new buses were purchased in either 1931 or 1932 but in 1933 came what was really a long-awaited development, namely a double-decker, progress being initiated through another demonstrator.

This machine was based on chassis number DDF 22500, possessed the invariable constant mesh gearbox, and was powered by a Gardner 6LW engine. Bodywork to the highbridge pattern was built by Beadle and had 52 seats. The assembly was registered as CG 3025 and appeared in the Stalybridge district in the early part of the year, although the first Daring, as the model was named, had been shown at the Olympia Motor Show of 1930.

The newcomer proved to be very successful and was purchased in the August for the round sum of £1,500 a figure which must be considered very favourable as it lasted until February 1948 and then realised £300 when sold for scrap, as bus number 144.

Having once proved that double-deckers were feasible the Board went further and ordered another batch but this time there was to be no nonsense about bodywork, it very predictably was built in Wigan and so in the December of 1933 came numbers 145 to 148 all of which looked similar but did in fact vary considerably under the skin.

Numbers 145 and 146 had Gardner engines at a chassis cost of £1,090 each but their sisters had a Thornycroft power unit of type DC 6 which reduced the cost by £120 per unit. These engines had the indirect injection combustion system and wet liners to the cylinders, and here was a major source of trouble for the top lands of the cylinder block castings were by no means as robust as they might have been. Tightening up the cylinder heads induced stresses which formed cracks and thus sealing was rendered well nigh impossible.

No real cure proved to be possible and so eventually both chassis (numbers 24291 and 24290 respectively) had Gardner engines installed but this proved to be a very troublesome business as the latter were about 6in longer than the original occupants of the engine bay and so the front bulkheads had to be set back by a like amount, a job needless to say that was undertaken at Wigan, not that the Board worried for the contract specified that if the DC 6 was not successful it would be replaced at the chassis manufacturers expense.

Up to this time bus starting had depended on a handle and the skill of the driver . . . or his strength but manual effort and a diesel engine were not compatible.

Consequently electric starters were incorporated plus a series/parallel switch giving 24 volts for starting or 12 volts for usual running/lighting purposes, a feature which was unique to the early Darings.

One more double-decker to the 6LW/Northern Counties pattern followed in 1934 number 149, but here is a mystery for the order sheets for 1934, copies of which were kindly provided by Messrs. Thornycroft, show five vehicles being called for and the chassis number of 149 is lower than those of 145 or 146 so why the 12 month delay before delivery?

Series manufacture was recommenced in 1935 when number 150 to 155 took the road at the reduced price of £1035 per chassis, despite the inclusion of a number of detail improvements together with the lengthening of the wheel base to 16 ft 3 in.

These vehicles proved to be highly satisfactory and so it was no surprise when repeat orders for 1936 were announced but what was surprising was the fact that no more would follow.

Thornycrofts had been surveying their production and had come to the conclusion that the firm should withdraw from the heavy duty passenger transport field a fact which gave rise to much local bewailing for the then existing combination of a Gardner engine and a simple but robustly constructed chassis was giving a very trouble-free service under two handicaps which are not present in 1972, namely tram track laced, cobbled road surfaces and a high percentage of newly trained ex-tramway drivers, for these 1935 orders were mainly for replacement purposes as the Roaches-Mossley-Ashton route closed on May 25 and the Ashton to Mottram and Stalybridge to Mossley via Millbrook services ended on June 29.

Numbers 156 to 159 comprised another four double deckers to the previous 16 ft 3 in wheelbase specification and at the even lower price of £980 per chassis which again had Northern Counties 48-seat highbridge bodies. They entered service on June 1, 1936 along with eight single-deckers numbers 160 to 167 inclusive that were needed for the Roaches route for whilst double-deck trams being firmly restricted to rails could negotiate Black Rock Bridge and its associated curves double-deck motor buses were not permitted to do so.

The Cygnet type 17 ft 4 in wheelbase chassis on which the latter were based had Gardner engines but this time of the smaller 5LW pattern, and carried most attractive bodies of metal-framed construction with 36 seats, well-rounded roofs, rotating ventilators and a single rear doorway which was fitted with a sliding door.

They also had, when new, forward-facing front seats which earned them special marks from this author who was not attracted to the SHMD habit of fitting some of its vehicles with a front seat of the rear-facing cross bulkhead form which was an absolute hazard to successful bus (or tram) spotting, but he then had no idea of what was to follow in the September of 1941 when all eight were converted to perimeter seating which gave each of the 30 passengers so accommodated no view at all and even less to the innumerable horde who crowded into the centre space thus made available for their use.

Number 121 also underwent the same process in October 1941 but it only lasted in this guise until June 30, 1943, when it was withdrawn, although it apparently was retained by the Board until final disposal in September 1945. This bus incidentally received an oil engine as late as the March of 1940.

He had first hand experience of all this for by 1932 he was living at the edge of SHMD territory and so was seeing all the changes detailed herein at first-hand but he much preferred either of these two seating layouts to what he came to find on the post Thornycroft era of double-deckers. Without any

The 300,000 mile Thornycroft bus at the Snake Inn, August 1935.

The last of the line. A Cygnet of 1936—actually 163 —shows off the shapely design of its metal-framed body.

The 52-seat Beadle-bodied demonstrator pictured in 1933 shortly before purchase by the Joint Board and repainting as 144.

doubt the favourite seat of most boys is on top at the front, but the Board seeking the modern image adopted streamline bodies with streamline paint styles and a front dome that was identical to the one at the rear both from a metal and glazing point of view. As a result the view forward from either of the outside seats was virtually non existent and this feature was to ruin many a bus ride until well after the war, in fact it is doubtful if he would ever have forgiven the Board had it not been for the Thornycroft policy and a surprising extension of it.

In 1932 that old adversary North Western took over most of the former Goodfellow concern that was based in Hyde and so came

to acquire seven BC type Thornycrofts. These were very much oddities in what was then a Tilling-Stevens fleet and so their early withdrawal was kept firmly in mind.

Rumour has it that Mr. Grundy, the then general manager, heard of this and as a result certain negotiations were conducted on certain non-transport premises, with the result that the Board obtained the lot for £48 each complete. This author in later years came to know Mr. Grundy well and having a high regard for his abilities and memory would think that in this instance at least fiction is truly fact, but what is certainly fact is that completeness did not last long.

The vehicles were received at Tame Valley

13

in the December of 1935 but then a contract was signed with Northern Counties for seven new bodies and off went the chassis to Wigan for resurrection to return later as numbers 85 to 91.

Despite the new bodies though they must by 1939 have become to be regarded as fully written down in value for numbers 85, 86, 87, 88, 90 and 91 were handed free of charge to the Local Authorities of Hyde, Mossley, Stalybridge, Dukinfield, Audenshaw, and Glossop in that order for Civil Defence duty. Only number 85 was ever returned and this was finally sold for scrap in 1946 when it realised £60, something over twice the value of the odd man out number 89 which went to the breakers in 1939.

These seven vehicles actually represented the second second-hand purchase for in December 1933 two other vehicles were obtained from the same source but at the lower figure of £25 each. Numbered 142 and 143 they came to the Board as its part of the Goodfellow business, for this transaction was a joint North Western/Manchester/SHMD affair, although the first-named company took the largest share.

Of the BC type with chassis number 17741 and 16314, registration numbers LG 271 and DK 5290 respectively, 143 met a sad end being totally destroyed by fire in July 1935 but 142 survived until the last day of December 1939. The writer has been told that both of these buses also received the four cylinder CI engine as a replacement for the original petrol unit but cannot confirm the veracity of this statement, although it is certain that they were fully overhauled before entering service in January 1934.

Other Thornycrofts also vanished in the early stages of the war such as 133, 139 and 140 whilst 142 became a tower wagon in 1942 and so by the middle of that year the Thornycroft sun was visibly setting, as only the 24 Gardner-powered Cygnets or Darings totalling 16 and 8 respectively remained.

When the marque finally went out of production experiments were made by the Board with Bristol, Leyland and Daimler buses but it would seem that the availability of the Gardner engine was a major selling point, as were the advantages offered by preselective transmission and so the Daimler was adopted as the new standard.

Yet again the first such bus to be purchased was a former demonstrator, registration number BWK 860, which had an MCW 56-seat metal framed body and entered the fleet in September 1936 as number 168, but as can be expected from previous history the first production batch numbers 169 to 179 that came out in the May of 1937 had more Northern Counties bodywork.

Thirty more Daimlers followed between 1937 and 1940 and eight more utilities, one with Brush and four with Massey coachwork were obtained in 1943.

Further rolling stock was unavailable for almost four years but in June 1947 postwar vehicles started to come into stock in quantity and the days of the "Thornies" were obviously numbered.

It was at this point, though, that one of those interesting "might have beens" that often enliven life occurred and the circumstances are worth detailing, for there rolled one morning into the Tame Valley depot of the Joint Board a BRAND NEW Thornycroft double-deck chassis.

The company had decided in that year to investigate the passenger market and produced the prototypes of a new range of heavy duty chassis which were intended both for single or double-deck work.

They were basically identical having a neat and rather attractive bonnet and radiator assembly that concealed a Thornycroft 7.88 litre six cylinder direct injection oil engine that produced 100 bhp at 1750 rpm.

This power was taken through a conventional fluid flywheel to the frame mounted gearbox and here was something new for some of the gear trains contained therein were of the synchromesh type but incorporated a self-shifting mechanism, the whole being referred to by the manufacturers as "the new transmission system", which was intended to give all the advantages of the preselector type of control from a gear box having more simplified internals than those found in the Wilson design. Could the SHMD preference have been an influencing factor here?

At the forward end of the main shaft was a small single dry plate clutch which had a clutch stop. The main and layshafts carried three trains of constant mesh gears and one set of sliding mesh which provided the emergency low ratio.

The constant mesh wheels were mounted on a concentric sleeve which terminated in an annulus with internal teeth with a connection to the output shaft via the synchromesh unit which had corresponding teeth arranged to act as engaging dogs.

In theory it all worked like this.

Under the steering wheel was a small preselector lever. If the bus was say on a rising gradient the driver selected bottom and depressed the accelerator pedal. The vehicle would begin to move forward until the propeller shaft came to the stage of over running the engine when the synchromesh unit moved forward to engage second automatically and at this point the driver had to push the selector lever into the third gear position.

When third was actually needed the accelerator was eased down and the pedal which controlled the front clutch depressed, momentarily when pressure could be reimposed on the throttle and with the propeller shaft again over-running the engine third would come in. Repeating the procedure produced top gear.

The declutching action was only necessary when going up the box, changing down simply involved selecting the required ratio and

Above: The new transmission, showing the control system. The lever under the steering wheel is for gear selection, the other for engaging reverse. The clutch pedal was only required when changing up or utilising reverse. *Below:* The second double-deck chassis as bodied by Thurgood, in August 1952.

then de-accelerating and then re-accelerating the power unit.

The rest of the chassis was of the simple construction so beloved of yore by the Joint Board with 16 in diameter drum brakes operated by air pressure, an open propeller shaft, a substantial worm drive axle unit, cam and roller steering, and reverse camber elliptical springs, but these welcome characteristics were not sufficient to overcome Stalybridge suspicions as to the desirability of the new transmission system, and it would seem that these were well-based in view of what happened later.

Two double-deck chassis had been built, which were numbered 48604 and 48605 and given the designation NR6/DG and the latter was sold that same year to Parrs of Leicester who fitted it with a saloon type of body. Its sister was kept around the factory until 1952 when it was sold to the associated firm of John I. Thornycroft of Woolston, Southampton, but by this time both had come to acquire more conventional five speed gearboxes for experience proved that initially preselection was uncertain whilst wear later could result in only the low ratio being obtainable.

The same fault needless to say was to be found in the single deck NR6/SG version which totalled five examples, all of which went to the Bristol Co-operative Society, were provided with coach bodies, and spent their lives on private hire work.

These seven machines though were not the sum total of the Thornycroft passenger experiment, for 1947 also saw the completion of two chassis each of types SG 8 and YF. The SGs were of similar construction to the aforementioned machines, had large bonnets, forward control, left hand drive, and by being built to the width of 8 ft were obviously intended for export. The YF on the other hand was a smaller version, being rather similar to the well-known Bedford lightweight forward control coach that was so popular in that early postwar period, and so obviously needed to be built in substantial numbers to achieve any commercial worth.

It would seem that the Basingstoke company came to the conclusion that success could better be achieved by concentrating on goods chassis for three of these last chassis were soon broken up, but the fourth, an SG 8, was transferred to the factory fleet and so made history by becoming the last double-deck Thornycroft of all, although alas it carried in this capacity not passengers but a double line of vehicle cabs from their assembly shop to the production line.

If that prototype chassis had possessed a conventional gearbox and a Gardner engine we could well have seen the placing of a Stalybridge order, for it was with seeming reluctance that withdrawals of the prewar survivors of the breed continued and it was not until March 31, 1952 that the last doubledecker number 159 of 1936 worked its last passenger duty.

Single-deckers continued to be around for some while longer but finally on October 30 of the same year number 164 completed its last service run and was then sold to a Stratford London firm for £125 and somehow or other the Stalybridge area has never quite seemed the same since.

Now of course neither the manufacturer nor the operator remains as a separate entity for the Thornycroft business was acquired firstly by AEC and later came into the British Leyland orbit to now form the Special Products Division of that vast Corporation, whilst SHMD was amalgamated into the Selnec passenger transport authority as from November 1, 1969, but I hope that these brief notes will have evoked some happy memories for those readers who knew the Tame Valley thirty or forty years ago and perhaps make the younger generation of bus spotters regret what they have missed.

Finally might I express my thanks to Mr. L. G. Stockwell, former General Manager of the SHMD undertaking who previously served on the staff of Thornycroft of Basingstoke, and to Mr. Sollett the General Manager of that company and his assistant Mr. Dascombe, three gentlemen who have provided many details about the buses and their characteristics that were previously quite unknown to me.

Municipal muster/1: East Anglia

Photographs by R. L. WILSON

Great Yarmouth 5, a 1937 Leyland TD5/Weymann, was still operating in 1959.

Great Yarmouth 43, one of four AEC Regent Vs with 61-seat Massey bodies bought in 1959.

Photographed in 1967, Ipswich 23 is a 1956 AEC Regent III with attractive Park Royal 61-seat body.

Foot of page: Another AEC/Park Royal combination in Ipswich, 1954 Regal IV 42-seater 12.

A 1959 scene in Lowestoft, featuring 6, a 1945 Guy Arab with rebuilt Massey utility body. Following is an Eastern Counties Leyland PD1A/ECW.

Foot of page: Colchester 48, one of a fleet of smart Massey-bodied Leyland PD2s.

Faced with the problem of low bridges, Southend has bought Alexander-bodied Leyland Lowlanders like 332 shown here.

Another solution to the low bridge problem were AEC/Park Royal Bridgemasters like 320.

Highland holiday

STEWART J. BROWN takes a farewell look at Scottish buses

Bedfords form a large proportion of the Highland fleet. This one is operating on the recently-improved road on the north shore of Loch Broom, between Ullapool and Braemore Junction.

Trying to see Scotland in seven days is considered to be the prerogative of the American tourist. I did it in July 1971 as a holiday for my wife and myself, combined with a farewell to buses in my native country which I was leaving to take up an overseas appointment.

We set off from Glasgow by car at 0900 on a sunny Saturday morning (not realising that we would see little more sun till our return to central Scotland six days later). We sped through Alexanders (Midland) territory making our first stop at Perth—our destination was Inverness by the most direct route. Just north of Perth I made a slight deviation from the main road to visit Spittalfield, home of A. & C. McLennan who is the largest independent operator north of Glasgow. McLennan's services cover a fairly large area centred on Perth, Blairgowrie and Dundee, but the tiny village of Spittalfield houses his workshops and principal depot and is always worth a visit.

This day was no exception and on the premises were Daimler double-deckers formerly owned by Aberdeen Corporation, and ex-Alexanders (Fife) Guy LUF semi-coaches, none of which had been prepared for service. The running fleet consisted of a few ageing coaches and ex-London RTLs. The RTLs were fitted with platform doors. However, pride of place went to the Guy Wulfrunian—the only one in Scotland—which had been purchased at the beginning of the year and never been operated in service; a navy blue/white elephant! Like most Wulfrunians it originated with West Riding.

Next stop was the tourist town of Pitlochry where we lunched and I paid a brief visit to Alexanders (Midland) most northerly depot whose fleet was principally Albion Vikings and Leyland Tiger Cubs. Fifty miles of open road brought us to Aviemore where Highland Omnibuses has a small sub-depot in the form of an open yard at the north of this village-cum-tourist town. The yard's sole occupant was a ski-bus—one of six Leyland bus-bodied Royal Tigers acquired from Ribble and subsequently converted by Alexanders (Coachbuilders) to carry skis in an open rear platform.

We arrived in Inverness in the late afternoon to find the town being served by the most colourful collection of buses to be operated by one company anywhere in Britain. The summer of 1971 saw Highland Omnibuses in a unique transitional stage having absorbed most of MacBrayne's services and part of Alexanders (Midland) territory, without having repainted acquired vehicles in its own livery (which had been changed anyway). So in Inverness there were buses in Highland's old maroon/cream livery; buses in the then new poppy red/peacock blue livery; coaches in the smart grey/blue colour scheme copied from a Manchester firm in 1965; ex-MacBrayne buses in Mac-Brayne's red/green/cream livery (which was nicer than it sounds); and ex-Midland buses in that company's blue/cream colours. There were even red/cream buses acquired from Western SMT but, alas, out of service!

Repainting of acquired buses was proceeding at a reasonable pace—the influx of Mac-Brayne and Midland buses had increased the Highland fleet from about 215 to about 310 vehicles. Many of the ex-MacBrayne vehicles were sold without being repainted but it still left Highland with a large number of vehicles in non-standard liveries. To present a uniform image for tours an effort was made to repaint all the ex-MacBrayne coaches (as opposed to buses) first—a task in which Alexanders (Northern) helped at their Aberdeen workshops. I saw only one ex-MacBrayne coach which was not repainted blue/grey; so this scheme must have worked well.

Highland operates a network of town services in Inverness using Bristol Lodekkas acquired from Scottish Omnibuses in 1963, and ex-Western SMT and Central SMT Albion Lowlanders. Short and long distance rural services cover the north of Scotland. These are operated by all types of vehicles (mainly Reliances, Bedfords and Fords). At the time of this visit ex-MacBrayne routes were generally being operated by ex-Mac-Brayne buses.

The next day was Sunday—a word to strike dread into the hearts of visitors to Scotland. The best thing to do on a Scottish Sunday is

Top to bottom: McLennan's Wulfrunian looked very smart—partly because it had done no work for its new owner; Highland's CD59, still in MacBrayne's livery and on an ex-MacBrayne service—the paye sign is a Highland addition; a Plaxton-bodied Bedford, new to MacBrayne in 1968, and now part of Highland's coach fleet.

22

Top to bottom: Buses outnumber people at John o'Groats—nearest the camera is a Ford bus, outside the hotel a Bedford dual-purpose vehicle, both with Duple Group bodies; a Highland Albion Lowlander in the striking new peacock blue/poppy red livery; two ex-Central SMT buses in the Highland fleet at Dounreay—a 1962 Lowlander and a 1955 Lodekka coach.

travel—and travel we did, to Thurso on the north coast (top right-hand corner on the Scottish map which you should have beside you). The road to Thurso took us via Dingwall where there is a large depot (by Highland standards) on the left as you enter the town from the south. I paused to inspect a pair of ex-Scottish Omnibuses AEC Reliance 590s then carried on to Struie (brief pause to admire as much of the scenery as could be seen through the mist) and Helmsdale (long pause to photograph McLeod's fleet).

McLeod of Helmsdale operates a school service between Helmsdale and Kinbrace. He had three vehicles at home when I passed which were, in order of size, a BMC minibus, a Strachans-bodied Ford Transit (pronounced Strakhans in Scotland, definitely not Strawns), and a Burlingham-bodied Bedford SB which must have been almost 20 years old and had been new to Scottish Omnibuses. All were painted blue/cream.

Our next stop was Wick, where we had Scottish Sunday Lunch—always an impressive meal and in our case tea and biscuits in the only cafe which was open! Like everything else, Highland's depot (by the railway station) was closed, so we continued north to Keiss (where there were two Bedfords belonging to Dunnett of Keiss) and John o'Groats which was typically . . . well, typically John o'Groats: there's no other description. Bleak, cold, miserable, and visited by tourists huddled in their cars and an Evangelical society trying to coax them out (with a noticeable lack of success); that's John o'Groats. Its only saving grace was two Highland vehicles—one on a tour and the other on service from Thurso. We then went to Dunnett Head, the most northerly point of the Scottish mainland which is considerably more attractive than John o'Groats. It however lacks buses, but you can't have everything! From there we did the last lap to Thurso.

There are three small independents in this corner of Scotland. Dunnett of Keiss, mentioned above, operates between Wick and John o'Groats; Morrison of Castletown connects Wick and Thurso via Lyth; and

Sutherland Transport's Lairg-Durness bus stops at Rhichonich for a transfer of mail. It is a Bedford VAS/SMT.

Allan of Spittal operates between Wick and Spittal and Spittal and Thurso. Allan does not provide a through facility from Wick to Thurso because on the days which he runs to Wick he does not run to Thurso and vice versa.

Thurso proved to be the most interesting Highland depot on this visit offering two Albion Lowlanders repainted in the poppy red/peacock blue livery (they looked magnificent!); the last remnants of the short-lived GL class (Guy Arab LUFs acquired from Western SMT); and one ex-MacBrayne Bedford VAS bus in an experimental red/cream livery which had been tried on two buses shortly after the MacBrayne take-over.

Monday was a holiday in Thurso, so we got off to an early start and headed west for Durness, taking the road via Janetstown with the intention of meeting the Thurso-bound bus of Peter Burr (Omnibuses) Ltd, which I knew we should pass. Unfortunately Janetstown (about two miles from Thurso) is so small that I passed through it unknowingly. I was about seven miles from Thurso still looking for Janetstown (and wondering how

the bus made the journey in ten minutes) when I met the bus on a corner and had to follow it back to Thurso to photograph it!

Peter Burr (Omnibuses) Ltd is a Highland subsidiary which until shortly before my visit owned one Bedford SB bus acquired from the independent Burr of Tongue. In July 1971 the company owned no vehicles but was operating the unique Highland Bedford VAM/Alexander mail bus which was exhibited at the 1965 Scottish Motor Show.

We restarted from Thurso at 1015, a bit behind schedule, and headed west once more, stopping at Dounreay Atomic Works to photograph some of the two-dozen Highland buses there (including an out-of-place Reliance in MacBrayne's livery) and then carrying on via Tongue to Durness (top left-hand corner of your map) passing only one empty Highland bus on the way. We then turned south

An ex-Alexanders (Midland) Reliance on the shores of Loch Ness, en route from Fort William to Inverness, in Highland's new standard livery.

for Kylesku ferry taking care not to miss the bus of Sutherland Transport which was due in Rhiconich just as we passed through. From Kylesku we continued to Ullapool via Lochinver—a tortuous road which enthusiastic motorists should not miss.

Sutherland Transport operates mail bus services centred on Lairg, where the buses connect with trains to and from Inverness. These services radiate from Lairg to Tongue, Durness, Scourie and Lochinver. Connecting minibus services are operated from Lochinver to Drumbeg by Matheson of Drumbeg, and from Tongue to Melness by Munro of North Talmine.

We spent Monday in Ullapool, then set off on Tuesday morning at 0930 after photographing the Ford Transit belonging to MacKenzie of Achiltibuie which operates from Achiltibuie to Ullapool where it connects with Highland's bus from Ullapool to Garve which in turn connects with trains to and from Inverness!

Highland's Ullapool to Garve bus left slightly earlier than we did; however we caught up with it and kept pace with it (it

was a high-speed VAS) to Braemore Junction, where it makes yet another connection with a minibus from Badluachrach operated by Taylor of Badcaul. At Braemore we left Highland's Bedford behind and headed for Muir of Ord, where I had the fortune to find an ex-Alexanders (Northern) Ford Thames/Duple coach operating on the five times daily service to Rosemarkie. This vehicle was one of four Ford coaches which Northern acquired from Simpson of Rosehearty and transferred to Highland.

Our route led back to Inverness once more where we stopped for lunch, then continued south along the banks of Loch Ness, heading for Fort William. On route we passed one of Highland's ex-Alexanders (Midland) Reliances operating a former MacBrayne journey on the Fort William to Inverness service. Things *do* get complicated!

Above: An ex-MacBrayne AEC Reliance/Park Royal-Roe, now with Highland. *Below:* One of two Albion Vikings acquired by Highland from Midland, at Oban.

A misty morning in Kilmartin with a MacDonald & MacLellan Bedford ready to leave for Lochgilphead.

Fort William was in an interesting state with MacBrayne services being operated by ex-MacBrayne buses, some of which were in Highland livery and some of which were still in MacBrayne's colours. Most of the services in and around Fort William were operated by AEC Reliances. Our destination was Oban and we stopped on the way at Ballachulish, where MacConnacher owns one Albion Nimbus/Plaxton coach which is used solely for hires.

At Oban English touring coaches outnumbered Scottish service buses, but what the latter lacked in quantity they made up in variety. Until late 1970 services in Oban were provided by Alexanders (Midland) and MacBrayne. Now they are provided by Highland using an odd mixture of vehicles including an ex-Midland Leyland Leopard, ex-Midland and ex-MacBrayne Reliances, ex-Midland Vikings, and an ex-MacBrayne Bedford VAS. At the time of this trip the aforementioned Leopard and some of the Reliances were still in Midland blue/cream livery, while one Viking and all of the ex-MacBrayne Reliances in the area were in Highland blue/grey coach livery. This looks fine on vehicles with large areas of blue, but unfortunately drab on the vehicles at Oban where grey was the predominant colour and blue was restricted to window surrounds.

On Wednesday morning we left Oban (which was typically wet) and continued our journey south. At Kilmartin (eleven miles north of Lochgilphead) I had the fortune to encounter an ex-Government Bedford SB belonging to Stag Garage of Lochgilphead operating on the Wednesday and Saturday only service from Lochgilphead to Ford. At Lochgilphead my arrival just after 1100 hours coincided with the arrival of the buses from Oban and Glasgow. In 1970 these would both have been MacBrayne buses. In 1971 the bus from Glasgow was a black/white Alexander-bodied Leopard of Western SMT (a standard type on the service since the day and hour of Western's takeover of the former MacBrayne route). The bus from Oban was an ex-Midland Reliance—in Midland livery—belonging to Highland who work the service

26

jointly with Western. Western's working (which will probably be withdrawn by the time this is published) was covered by an ex-MacBrayne Bedford VAS, in MacBrayne livery, owned by Highland, and hired to Western. Try working that lot out!

A Ford Transit minibus belonging to MacLachlan of Tayvallich (whose business was for sale in early 1971) was sitting in Lochgilphead having come in from Tayvallich on his service. In recent years MacLachlan has operated a variety of buses seating around 20 passengers—a Morris Commercial, a Thornycroft and a Bedford OLAZ. The fact that a Transit now suffices perhaps shows that just as small buses have grown more sophisticated (and expensive)—compare the OB and VAS type Bedfords—minibuses have also grown more sophisticated, more expensive, and bigger. The latter fact is often overlooked. And of course, passenger traffic has reduced. The only other bus in the vicinity was Stag Garage's unusual Austin with 14-seat body by Scottish Co-operative Wholesale Society. New in 1965 this was one of the last small buses (as opposed to minibuses) to enter service in Scotland. I suspect that it had arrived from Ormsary at 1100 hours on Stag Garage's other service which operates daily except Sunday.

From Lochgilphead we went down the Mull of Kintyre to Campbeltown, headquarters of West Coast Motor Services which runs a smart fleet of red/maroon/cream buses. West Coast recently absorbed the other Campbeltown operator, MacConnachie. MacConnachie operated two double-deckers for a while but the West Coast fleet is entirely single-deck. Services are operated from Campbeltown to Southend, Machrihanish and Carradale and a town service is provided in Campbeltown.

The most interesting service is Campbeltown to Tarbert with connections for Glasgow, Oban, Farlie and the islands of Arran and Islay, to quote the company's timetable. Briefly, the 0715 NSu from Campbeltown to Tarbert connects at Tarbert with a Western SMT bus to Glasgow (in MacBrayne's days there was a through ser-

One of the four MacBrayne Bedfords taken over by Western SMT awaits the Glasgow bus for the transfer of mail, at Rest-and-be-Thankful.

Left: This Willowbrook-bodied Reliance of West Coast was operating on the Campbeltown town service. *Right:* Gorman of Dunoon owns this BMC 250JU minibus.

One of the older ex-Central SMT Bedfords operated in Dunoon.

vice). The 1000 NSu from Campbeltown to Tarbert connects with a ferry to the islands of Islay, Gigha and Jura (certain days only); a Western SMT bus to Glasgow, which in turn connects at Lochgilphead with a Highland bus for Oban, and a steamer to Brodick (Arran) and Fairlie (on the Ayrshire Coast). Similar facilities are provided on journeys from Tarbert to Campbeltown.

The West Coast fleet consists of a variety of modern Bedfords—SB, VAS and VAM models. The most unusual is an SB with Yeates body and front entrance conversion (with the entrance ahead of the front axle). I saw only three non-Bedford buses—a Tiger Cub acquired from MacConnachie, a Royal Tiger ex-Leicester City Transport (which was out of service) and a Willowbrook-bodied

AEC Reliance previously in the fleet of Smith of Barrhead. This vehicle was operating the Town Service.

We returned to Ardrishaig to spend Wednesday night, pausing briefly at Tarbert to inspect West Coast Motor's garage. Western SMT now use the old MacBrayne Ardrishaig garage (as a sub-depot of Thornliebank, Glasgow) to house a few black/white Leopards and one ex-MacBrayne Bedford C type with Duple coach body (with mail compartment).

On Thursday, our last day in the Highlands, we set off early to be at the Rest-and-be-Thankful, on the Ardrishaig to Glasgow road, at 1045. At this time a Western Leopard from Glasgow bound for Tarbert connects with one of Western's ex-MacBrayne Bedford

VASs which operates between the Rest-and-be-Thankful and Carrick Castle. As there are only four Bedfords in the Western fleet this was reason enough to make the journey. I arrived at the appointed hour, and so did the two buses—accompanied by the heaviest rain we met on holiday. I did some quick picture-taking and was soaked to the skin.

From here we headed for Dunoon (with heaters on for drying purposes) getting slightly lost on our route to Tighnabruaich in the Kyles of Bute. Gorman of Dunoon operates a few services in the Tighnabruaich area, but when I arrived there was little to see —one Bedford coach in his garage, and a BMC minibus labelled Tighnabruaich sitting unattended near the main street. Of Gorman's services two are school days only, one is subject to alteration to connect with steamer services and one is daily (July and August), weather permitting. Quite a timetable!

At Dunoon there have been a few changes in recent years. Local services formerly operated by Dunoon Motor Services using elderly double-deckers are now operated by Cowal Motor Services using reasonably modern coaches. Coach tours which were previously operated by Alex Baird using modern second-hand coaches and Gold Line using new coaches are now all operated by Baird—still using modern second-hand coaches, most of which came from Central SMT. Baird and Cowal are owned by the same

person and most of the vehicles are in Central SMT's two-tone blue livery, although at the time of my visit consideration was being given to using the old Gold Line red/gold livery for coaches (i.e. Baird's fleet) and the two-tone blue livery for the Cowal "bus" fleet.

Cowal Motor Services operates an extensive network of services in and around Dunoon. To the casual observer the services seem somewhat "peaky"—for example five buses departing at 1500, one bus at 1515, then another mass exodus at 1530. For passengers this sort of system has an advantage in that the times are easily remembered. (Because the buses go different ways timetable co-ordination is unimportant). Bus enthusiasts have to be careful to be at the right place at the right time or they will miss the lot. The most interesting vehicle at Dunoon belonged to Gorman—an ex-Western Welsh Reliance with unusual Weymann coach body.

We had intended to leave Dunoon by car ferry for Gourock, however, the sight of slight waves put that notion out of my head and we left by road, passing the Rest-and-be-Thankful again where by luck Western's Bedford was waiting to make its afternoon connection in slightly brighter weather than had prevailed that morning. If I can stretch the Highlands just a little, at Arrochar I stopped to inspect the fleet of MacTavish—four ex-MacBrayne vehicles, with late 1950s Duple bodies and a Park Royal-bodied Maudslay which was out of use. A fitting close to a highland holiday which was partly a farewell to MacBrayne.

Prewar panorama

Photographs and commentary by G. H. F. ATKINS

Although this all-Leyland Lion was painted in the full East Midland yellow/cream/brown livery, it bore Leyland Motors name on the side. Nottingham, September 1934.

This must have been one of the earliest "gearless" buses. A Chesterfield all-Leyland Tiger of Chesterfield Corporation, March 1934.

A lucky shot, on a half-day trip to London in August 1935. London Transport Q3, an AEC Q with MCW body, at Victoria.

An all-Leyland Titan of Lincolnshire leaves Skegness for Boston, in June 1939.

Facing page, top: An evening scene at Victoria Coach Station, with a Western SMT Leyland Tiger/ Burlingham ready to leave for Glasgow, August 1937.

Above: This was the first style of body introduced by G. J. Rackham for the new Tigers. Sheffield Corporation all-Leyland TS1, in September 1934.

Centre: These two were seen together most nights in Huntingdon Street, Nottingham at 8.30 pm. Both are Leyland Tigers, one from East Midland, the other Lincolnshire. January 1937.

Below: The loaning of Corporation buses was extensively practised in the height of the summer season in the 1930s, and Nottingham vehicles were regular visitors to Mansfield, Derby and Grantham. Doncaster was a bit unusual. This Nottingham AEC Reliance/Short was photographed in July 1936.

Below: A "gearless" Leyland Tiger of West Riding, at Barnsley in June 1936.

A United Bristol B/United at South Cliff, Scarborough in June 1930. The United livery at this date was the same as East Midland, yellow/cream/brown.

United bodies for small private operators were fairly common in 1929—there were two others near this one, each with a different owner. It is a Leyland Tiger TS1 of J. Mitchell, Derby, at Skegness in July 1929.

I like this picture as it shows off to perfection the modified and very handsome radiator—now a thing of the past, alas! It was a United Leyland Tiger with Eastern Counties body, at Lincoln, August 1933.

Under new colours

Reorganisation in South Wales

The reorganisation of the National Bus Company has been noticeable all over the country, but few areas have seen so many changes as South Wales. In the east of the area, the Rhondda Transport Company was absorbed by the Western Welsh Omnibus Company Ltd., although, as both companies had worked together closely for several years, the visible signs of the change have been few. All vehicles quickly received Western Welsh legal lettering, but no effort was made to change the fleetnames other than on vehicles transferred to Western Welsh garages—indeed a few Western Welsh vehicles received Rhondda fleetnames!

Most drastic action was taken with the vehicles formerly owned by Neath & Cardiff Luxury Coaches Ltd. which ceased operation on December 31, 1970. Most of their fleet passed to the South Wales Transport Company Ltd., but six coaches were taken over by Western Welsh.

However, it is in the Swansea area that the biggest changes have taken place. Not only have Thomas Brothers (Port Talbot) and United Welsh been merged with South Wales Transport but the last-named company has been forced by financial difficulties to sell modern vehicles, cancel orders for new vehicles and replace them by second-hand vehicles from other NBC operators.

D. G. Bowen

Once number 9 in the United Welsh coach fleet, this Bristol MW6G/ECW is now South Wales bus 386.

This 1955 Tiger Cub/Weymann is now South Wales 304, although it still had Thomas Bros. livery when photographed in November 1971.

One of three Bristol RELL/ECW buses ordered by United Welsh but delivered direct to South Wales. It was photographed on service 116 at Llanmorlais in the Gower.

A former Neath & Cardiff AEC Reliance/Plaxton coach, now Western Welsh 106.

This ex-Midland General Bristol Lodekka became 908 in the South Wales fleet, and is seen at Aberavon, awaiting its departure time for Swansea.

Have they fixed the where and when?

JOHN PARKE remembers the pleasures of prewar Cornwall

Although one saw little of bus operation in the Duchy of Cornwall until the summer which tailed off into the 1939–45 War, that visit had great interest from both operational and vehicular viewpoints. So far as the latter were concerned there was still quite a number of types which had largely vanished from other parts of the country with which one was acquainted and the major operator, Western National, had kept in service a fairly varied fleet including units from acquired operators. So far as actual facilities were concerned there were considerable contrasts with a considerable number of market-day type services by both independents and WNOC, a good many regular services by the latter and a few by the former and some unexpectedly substantial operations to the docks at Falmouth and works at Camborne and Redruth. In the variety of all these operations lay the reason for the title of this article which comes from R. S. Hawker's *Song of the Western Men* and continues:

> *And shall Trelawny die?*
> *Here's twenty thousand Cornish men*
> *Will know the reason why!*

The last line too has an apposite application to this theme.

The first line was, however, singularly relevant for while there were in those days comprehensive local timetables for rail and bus services—often sponsored by the local newspaper—and produced very tidily on their behalf by Index Publishers, they were by no means complete. This was seldom if ever the fault of the compiler or publisher since many of the operators disclosed alterations belatedly if at all and there were also some cases where they felt it quite unnecessary to notify the traffic commissioners either. It followed that it was not always easy to know times of owners in whom one was interested and it was really reasonable to ask "have they fixed the where and when?" By that time the Omnibus Society had commenced the publication of lists of independents and their routes by traffic areas and the first of these had been assembled most efficiently by John Corner, one of its younger members who was unfortunately destined not to return from the War. Obviously much of his material was derivable from applications in *Notices & Proceedings* but these were not always so helpful when renewal was sought without modification and there was merely a reference back to the original grant. One solution was to write to the operator concerned and this is

N. A. Whitfield's Thornycroft Dainty JY 6129, in Truro.

Pendennis, Falmouth ex-SMT Leyland Lion and Thornycroft Dainty at Falmouth Docks.

Western National Bedford, CTA 540 at Lands End in 1939.

A vintage line up at Lemon Quay, Truro. Julian (Ideal) Gilford 168 OT, Majestic (Bennetts) Daimler CF6 and Bedford.

where the other line of the poem comes into it for, while it was not 20,000, several operators wrote back asking why this information was sought and one went on to add that there were too many "forriners" coming to Cornwall as it was. Undaunted by such recalcitrance John worked on and most helpfully the list appeared before we went west and, indeed, provided added incentive for going. It should perhaps be added at this point that, so far as Truro was concerned, the mystery was solved to some extent by the *Cornish Almanac* which was recommended by a local newsagent and proved to have a page devoted to bus services amid a large amount of information anent local dishes, monuments and other matters.

Falmouth was, and is, a pleasant place in which to stay even if it is no longer possible as it was that first time to see a couple of grain ships come in, anchor in the bay and then next evening sail again with the red of the setting sun colouring the full spread of their sails. There was colour ashore as well with 16 operators working into Falmouth and four of them actually maintaining the local service between the main bus terminus at the Moor and Gyllyngvase Beach from which it was easy to see the ships. This service was worked only from June 1 to September 30 and two of its operators—Lewis Motors (Falmouth) Ltd and S. L. Taylor—had no other stage services, although as Silver & Haywoods Tours and Cornish Riviera Tours respectively they were the two major independent operators of excursions and tours from Falmouth. Taylor's Garage was the Morris agent in the town so there was some reason for most of the fleet being of Morris-Commercial manufacture including two RPs, a Leader and two 12-seat all-weather coaches on the 2-ton chassis which had recently entered service. The bus service was normally worked by a Dennis G. The beach service was maintained on a rota basis and the other partners were C. N. Rickard who had started

Banfil, Mawnan Smith's Dodge, CV 5061 at Falmouth Quay.

Mrs L. M. Hearle (Riviera) Dennis Ace at Falmouth.

services in March 1912 as the Penryn & Falmouth Motor Company and Western National. The latter had made its debut on the route the previous summer when it had taken over Rider's Garages Ltd. This firm had a convenient garage at the Moor, its share in the beach service and a group of excursions and tours.

Eight years had by then elapsed since the taking effect of the 1930 Traffic Act and conditions were, in the main, pretty orderly. The road between Falmouth and Penryn via Greenbank which had long been the scene of intense rivalry was maintained on a rota system by five operators: the Carol service of Harry & Tonkin, C. H. Kinsman, C. N. Rickard (mentioned earlier), A. C. Rogers & Sons, and the Duchy Cars of H. Thomas. A sixth operator, Mrs M. Hosking & Sons, had faded out in 1938 after the lady had died and there had been a somewhat undignified scramble for her licence for that route and another between the Moor and Swanvale. One was not to know it at the time but the Duchy Cars service was destined to come off in August 1939 after Rogers had covered them

for a month in the emergency. The times were shared between the other partners on the route. The Duchy bus, a 20-seat Willys, certainly looked as if it had seen better days. Nor was the Penryn road the end of joint endeavour for there were three operators plying between Falmouth and Mylor. One was Western National which ploughed on regardless and followed a slightly different route and the others were Pelere Motors (W. J. George) and Riviera Service (Mrs L. M. Hearle). Mr George had begun with a Falmouth-Stithians route in 1927 but had found this unrewarding, although he had retained a Monday service from Carclew to Helston via Stithians, Carnkie and Porkellis and a Wednesday service from Flushing to Truro via Mylor, Carclew, Devoran, Stickling Bridge and Carnon Downs. He had a somewhat mixed fleet which included a recently-withdrawn Willys, a Reo, a small Thornycroft ex-GWR and Western National, two Commer Invaders and later a Gilford 1680T and a 166SD of the same make to replace the Thornycroft and the Reo. His timetable for the Mylor-Falmouth service was almost iden-

Penryn & Falmouth Gilford AS6 (ex-Robson, Smeltingsyke) at Falmouth Moor in 1941.

Truro in 1939, with Western National Bedfords, Dennis Ace and Bristol J.

tical with that of Mrs Hearle and carried a note to the effect that it was "operated in conjunction with the Riviera service" on Tuesdays and Thursdays. When, on a wartime visit, I got to know him I asked what this meant in fact, he replied that it all depended on circumstances and that sometimes one worked the morning journeys and the other the afternoon ones. At that time Mrs Hearle's operations, which were later to become Riviera Services Ltd and absorb Lewis Motors, were maintained with a smartly-kept Dennis Ace emanating from Whiteley Bros operating as Glenway in the Halifax area.

Another independent dating back to the early 1920s was F. Howard, operating as Pendennis Motors, and by then concentrating on a daily service through very sparse country between Falmouth and Camborne via Penryn, Long Downs, Carnkie, Penmarth, Nine Maidens and Troon. He had begun with a Falmouth-Truro service which had caused Cornwall Motor Transport a mort of trouble but turned in due course to opening up a new road. He also had a workers service between Swanvale and Falmouth Docks.

There was an elderly Thornycroft BC but in 1939 most operations were with a Thornycroft Dainty purchased new and a Gilford AS6 to which had just been added two Leyland Lion LTs still in their SMT blue. Another operator of some length of tenure was Martin Bros, of Ponsanooth near Perranwell, with a weekday service between Porthtowan (Beach) and Falmouth Docks via St Day, Carharrack, Ponsanooth and Penryn. The route was worked also on Sundays from mid-July to the end of September and other services were one on Fridays from Carharrack to Redruth via St Day and Vogue and a summer Wednesday and Sunday operation from Ponsanooth to Perranporth via Carharrack, St Day, Scorrier and Blackwater. All vehicles seen were Reos and their state is best described as marginal. The routes with modifications, were to be sought by Western National in the summer of 1946.

One of the newest independent vehicles to be seen working into Falmouth that summer was a Bedford WTB with Willmott bodywork owned by E. H. Manley (Lannarth Tours), of Lanner, near Redruth. Somewhat surprisingly

A Western National Dennis Mace at Truro (Public Rooms) in 1939.

Two Western National Bristols at Lands End in 1939.

the service was confined to dock workers, surprising that is in view of its modernity compared with most of those to be seen outside the docks at knocking-off time. Some two years later this business passed to H. N. Trewren, also of Lanner, who had already established a number of services which he operated under the fleetname Marigold. These included a workers service to Falmouth Docks from Redruth with journeys at other times to Falmouth (Moor) on a Tuesday and Thursday service from Frogpool, a Tuesday and Friday route from Redruth to Devoran via Lanner, Frogpool and Bissoe and Saturday services from Redruth to Peace via Buller Hill and Carnkie and to Truro via Lanner, Frogpool, Twelveheads, Bissoe, Baldhu and Hugus. There were six through journeys each way on the last.

There were also summer services on certain days to the beaches at Porthtowan and Perranporth. Marigold is still operating. At that time its fleet was somewhat mixed but

several vehicles such as a Bedford WTB and a Dennis Ace were fairly new and all were well-kept including a rare bird in the shape of a 20-seat Mercedes-Benz previously in service with Lang, of Bideford. The other second-hand vehicle seen was an ex-Devon General Leyland Tiger TS1. Operating as Noel, J. O. Whear, of Tuckingmill, provided a workers service to Falmouth Docks from Camborne via Redruth and Lanner.

Two other operators were based to the west of Falmouth. One was E. G. Banfil (later to become Banfil & Barrington), of Mawnan Smith, with a Thurgood-bodied Dodge working between Trebah and Falmouth by a rather more inland route than that followed by Western National. Trebah is known also as Helford Passage and it was probably due to this confusion that the local timetable managed to repeat exactly similar details of the service twice in its 1937 issues. The other operator, with a Bedford WLB that had a relatively rare Grose body, was W. J. Bowden,

A Western National Leyland Lioness on the coach stand at Truro (Lemon Bridge) in 1939.

A Western National Leyland Lion PLSC ex Dunn's, Taunton, with its third body, on the Gyllyngvase Beach service in Falmouth after the war.

of Higher Tregoney, near Constantine. All four routes began at Constantine. That on Mondays was to Helston via Gweek, Wednesdays saw a journey to Truro via Port Navis, Mawnan, Treverva, Mabe and Norway Inn, Fridays a Redruth service via Rame Cross, Carnkie, Penmarth, Nine Maidens and Four Lanes, and Saturdays a Falmouth operation via Dreva Mill and Treverva.

Despite this plethora of independent facilities, Western National found plenty of occupation with two services from Falmouth to Penzance via Helston, of which 21 went via Penryn and 22 via Constantine and Gweek, regular services to Truro and to Redruth and also to Trebah (Helford Passage) and that already mentioned to Mylor. Across the other side of harbour was a most interesting service which was worked on two days a week between St Mawes and Truro. The attraction lay in its use of King Harry's Ferry to cross the River Fal an operation which restricted the type of vehicle that could be used and

was later avoided by adopting another route.

The main market day in Truro was Wednesday and the majority of independents—except the aforementioned Marigold—worked there on that day and in many cases on Saturday as well. To one who was little acquainted with the place an overall survey was not easy There was the problem of timetables which was mentioned earlier and there was also the fact that about four different terminals were used even allowing for the habit of some operators of calling the same place by different names. As for indulging in photography this was almost impossible. One tried, but several points, such as High Cross near the cathedral, were surrounded by comparatively tall buildings and all that one can do is to sigh heavily over dim views and try to decipher the main features of some examples of what were, even then, almost veteran vehicles.

There were delightful fleetnames. W. A. Tremain who ran in from Cubert and

Above left: James, Grampound Road Dodge at Truro (Lemon Quay) in 1941. *Above:* Mrs Lidgey (The Fal) Bedford at Lemon Quay.

A Pendennis, Falmouth Leyland Lion, ex-Devon General.

Crantock by various routes did so as One and All Bus Service. It is moreover impossible to avoid setting down the intermediate points on one of the services which were Rejjerrah, Goonhavern, Wheal Francis, Zelah (the Tremain base) and Allet. A BAT formerly in the fleet had gone, but there was a Surrey-Dodge—Cornwall seemed full of Dodges—and a Morris-Commercial Viceroy. Rather less out of the ordinary were the Reliance Service of Harper, Son & Kellow from St Agnes via Penstraze and Highertown and Ideal Motor Services of G. Julian & Son, Grampound Road. The latter worked each weekday from Treviscoe via St Stephens, Menna, Brighton and Ladock and according to its return to Motor Transport Year Book had two Albions, two Reos and a Chevrolet, but one was hardly surprised that the buses seen were a Bedford, two Fords and a Gilford 1680T. The City of Truro business of A. Richards had passed to Western National in 1938, but another Richards—W. E.—who plied as Truronian Cars was working on Wednesdays to Chacewater and on that day and Saturday to St Michael Penkivel via Tresillian and Merther with two Chevrolets and a Morris-Commercial RP ex-London Transport. A. & G. Morse, of Veryan, operated as Roseland Motors. Its service to Portloe was worked jointly with E. J. Tregunna on Mondays, Wednesdays and Saturdays and it must be admitted that its only direct connection with the beautiful Roseland peninsula was on summer Tuesdays with a service between Portloe and Percuil. It made a marked contrast with the scenery on the Friday service from Portloe to St Austell! Another three-days-a-week operation was that of the Fal Service of Mrs E. Lidgey working from Ruan Lanihorne via Tregoney, Trewarthenick, Probus and Tresillian.

Another operator based, like Ideal, on Grampound Road was James Bros operating as the Dove Service on Wednesdays and Saturdays to Truro via Grampound, Probus and Tresillian and on Fridays to St Austell. As it happened one saw in Truro the normal-control Gilford of H & P Rosewarne which was based on Porthleven, near Helston. The route was from Ashton via Porthleven, Helston, Camborne and Scorrier and other services were from Portlheven to Penzance on Thursdays and to Redruth on Fridays. Applications by Western National to acquire were already in the pipeline and one believes that it may well have been the last Rosewarne operation. With a single Chevrolet 14-seater bearing the fleetname Blue Bird—there were at that time at least five operators in the Western Traffic Area using it—E. H. Thomas, of Trevellas, near St Agnes, had the customary Wednesday and Saturday working to Truro via Mithian and Sticklers Corner and a Friday service to Redruth via Mithian, Blackwater and Mount Ambrose and another Chevrolet owner was J. H. Trenhaile working from Feock, just off the Truro-Falmouth road, over a route served also by the WNOC. Subsequently the Trenhaile operation passed to R. A. Richards, of Truro. The last service to mention is also one that subsequently changed hands. It was that of N. A. Whitfield from Goonhavern to Truro via Rose and Callestick whereon a Mumford-bodied Thornycroft Dainty had yet to replace the Commer Invader that had seen long service. The business was later to be bought by S. R. Mitchell, of Perranporth.

One would expect Western National to be strong with the old-established routes that it had inherited from Cornwall Motor Transport and Cornish Buses. At that time its group of services commenced mostly at Public Rooms where space was somewhat limited. Those to such points as Falmouth, Newquay, Perranporth, Redruth and St Austell were daily and frequent with less frequent services to Bodmin and other points. There are still independent operators in Cornwall, some of them replacing Western National facilities which have been withdrawn in the past two years, and another thing which seems to remain unchanged is the problem of finding out have they fixed the why and when? It could be that the Government ideas of relaxing licensing controls, if carried through will have intensified the difficulty by the time these recollections are read.

Island buses

Photographs by R. L. WILSON

A MacBraynes Bedford VAS leaves Staffin village,
at the very north of Skye, in 1966.

Above: Two Manx Bedfords, W. H. Shimmin's MAN 610 and A. E. Clague's 2587 MN at Ramsey.
Below: A Bedford/Plaxton of Carson, Dunvegan, on the road to Bracadale, Skye.

Above: Prewar Douglas Corporation AEC Regent at Douglas Pier, withdrawn in 1967 but now preserved. *Below:* A Southern Vectis Bristol Lodekka at Yarmouth, Isle of Wight.

Above: An ex-Burton Guy of Thomas, at Barry Island—now joined to the mainland by a causeway. *Below:* Barrow Corporation Leyland Leopard on Walney Island in 1964.

Isle of Man Road Services 4, an all-Leyland PD1 at Onchan Head, Douglas, in 1964.

A similar vehicle, Western SMT RD342, at Rothesay, on the Isle of Bute, in 1964.

Daimlers on their home ground

Photographs by T. W. MOORE

Busmen have often been suitably patriotic in their choice of vehicles, like Albions in Scotland, AECs in London, Dennises in south-east England and Leylands in Lancashire. Daimlers have, naturally, had a strong hold in the Midlands. Home town Coventry has— apart from a momentary lapse when Leylands were bought—concentrated on Daimlers for many years, and Midland Red, West Midlands pte and most of the municipalities in the area have large Daimler fleets.

Above: Leaning over with the camber of the road in Derby, a Blue Bus Daimler CD650 picks up passengers.

Left: A Daimler CSG6-30—a rare breed of Daimler. A small number were employed by the Leicester Corporation fleet between 1959 and 1971. Metro-Cammell built the bodywork.

One of the immaculate Roe-bodied Daimler CVG6s of the 1957 era placed in service with Northampton Corporation.

Above: A Daimler CVD6 never seen in passenger service is this mobile printing unit owned by *The Birmingham Post and Mail.* It was new in 1951, with coachwork by Willisden Coachbuilders, Solihull.

Left: One of the Burton Willowbrook-bodied Daimler Fleetline single-deckers picks up passengers in Trinity Street.

51

A 1966 Midland Red Alexander-bodied Daimler Fleetline operating rural services between Leamington Spa and Bishops Tachbrook.

Above: A Metro-Cammell bodied Daimler Fleetline
delivered to Nottingham in 1966 approaches the
town centre. *Below:* One of the 1971 Trent
Alexander-bodied Daimler Fleetlines seen at
Derby bus station.

Coventry Transport's first one-man operated
Fleetline, with ECW body, in Broadgate.

A Derby Daimler CVG6 with Roe body in the
Market Place, Derby in 1970.

Seats on top in several languages

ROBERT E. JOWITT looks at a spreading British Tradition

Foreigners, we believe, have certain ideas about what are the particular attributes or features of Great Britain, imagining that it consists entirely of thick fog, the Queen, unreasonable licensing hours, and double-decker buses. These pages are not the place to discuss the truth or merits or otherwise of the first three; but there would appear to be a certain amount of accuracy in the statement that foreigners regard double-deckers as British Traditions, if we are to judge by the way that foreign students on British buses invariably charge up the stairs with much delight and even more noise.

However, on the Continent of Europe—even if the taverns stay open in more civilised fashion—fog is not unknown, there is a reigning queen and various kings' wives, and there are even double-decker buses here and there.

On the Continent the nearest likeness to the traditional red London Transport double-

Left: Almost an English scene. But this traditional English double-decker, though painted in a London Transport shade of red, is in fact in Bilbao, and is a second-hand London trolleybus.

Above: A modern Basque double-decker, as bizarre as the primitive types. This runs to the fringes of Bilbao.

decker is the traditional red London Transport double-decker—only it is a second-hand London Transport trolleybus.

Of numerous London trolleybuses in Spain, those in Bilbao look most like what they used to look like, because they are still red. Of course they have had their stairs and entrance altered to conform to the Spanish rule of the road, as have all Spanish ex-London trolleybuses; but in the other cities, such as Zaragoza and Tarragona, where these vehicles run, they have been painted in various bright Spanish colours. Perhaps red is too dangerous in a land of fighting bulls.

Two of the Bilbao specimens are of peculiar interest, in that they have been converted into diesel buses, and lengthened, with the result that they are far more impressive than ordinary London double-deckers.

Bilbao may also boast some genuine Spanish double-deck motor buses. Nearly all Iberian double-deckers are British built, or obviously influenced by British design, but

the independent operators round Bilbao have built according to their own feelings; Basque double-deck buses are almost as original as is Gaudi's Catalan architecture on the other side of the isthmus.

It may be noted at this juncture that the Catalan double-deckers are no longer with us. Barcelona boasted, at one time or another, double-deck trams, motor buses, trolleybuses and petrol-electric buses, of both British and Catalan types; but they are all gone now. Incidentally there was a report, in one of those very erudite weekend journals which delight in scandal and Raquel Welch, saying that Gaudi was knocked down and killed by a Barcelona trolley-bus. Gaudi's death was in 1926, and trolleybuses were not introduced in Barcelona until 1940. So how much is true of what they say about Raquel Welch?

Apart from the erstwhile Catalan double-deckers, the still-extant Basque double-deckers, and the ex-London trolleybuses, the rest of the double-deckers in Iberia are, as

57

A dog idling in a rather risky situation in Oporto.
A Leyland Atlantean looms large in the background.

mentioned above, fairly British, except for having entrances on the right, or wrong side; also, while certain of them are right-hand drive so that the driver sits above the gutter, certain of them are left-hand drive, and in the case of such buses as AECs with half-cabs, they look as if they were being seen in a mirror.

With cabs on one side or the other, or, in the case of newer buses, full fronted, these familiar looking buses wander about the alien streets of such places as Madrid, Oporto, Coimbra, and Lisbon; so far as the Portuguese examples are concerned, they run in company with splendidly antique tramcars—but the tramcars are single-deck, and therefore beyond the terms of reference of this opus.

Oporto also·runs some very modern and British-looking double-decker trolleybuses, in much the same colour as the Portsmouth trolleybuses; almost a port wine colour.

In Lisbon there are, besides the British double-deckers, some double-deckers known as Cityrama. These are sight-seeing coaches.

So we will pass on.

Only to find, in Paris, more Cityrama coaches. Also another breed of double-deck sight-seeing coach known as Paris Vision. The title suggests anything from Ingres' *La Source* to the Place Pigalle, and smacks certainly of femininity and possibly of beauty, depending on whether vision means the sort that Dante had, or the sort the butler saw; in point of fact the butler would pass by this vision quite unmoved, and Dante would probably think it very ugly. But it seems very popular among tourists.

The Cityrama coaches look like what the artist of Dan Dare in the 1950s thought buses might look like in 1999; we are inclined to think his prophecies incorrect. The Paris Visions look like ordinary single-deck French coaches—the sort that pick up Algerians in the Place Clichy on race-day mornings to take them to Longchamps—with something on the roof; there is no adequate description for this excrescence.

Adding upper decks on to buses in Paris seems to be a habit. It may be found even

among the Paris buses proper—or perhaps improper, now that all the open-back buses are scrapped; at all events, the Regie Autonome des Transports Parisiens sports in its fleet of standard buses a certain number (26 to be precise) of buses which differ from the rest merely by having an upper deck; as far as the top of the lower deck they are just the same, above the top of the lower deck there is . . . well, perhaps it is a vision. . . .

There is perhaps a certain justification for double-deckers in Paris, for the first motor buses of the Compagnie Generale des Omnibus, in 1906, were double-deckers. These, like the present generation, were of slightly bizarre appearance, the lower deck being a traditional horse-bus type body, while the upper deck was roofed but open-sided, as on the contemporary trams: self-contained steam cars, compressed-air cars, and accumulator cars. The double-decker trams were better-looking than the double-decker buses. But both trams and buses had that necessary Paris feature which is sadly lacking on the new buses—the open rear platform.

Paris is the fairest city in the world, but Vienna runs it a fairly close second. Vienna swarms with trams, which may, from certain points of view, make it even fairer than Paris, not that the present day trams are by any means so charming as the Hapsburg and Strauss trams. It is the policy in Vienna, however, to replace certain tramlines with buses, because they are in narrow streets, or because they are not sufficiently patronised, or because of any number of anti-tram and probably prejudiced arguments. While the scrapping of tramlines is entirely to be deplored, a degree of merit can none the less be found in the substituting buses on route 13; whether these take up less space than the trams is doubtful, for they are enormous; and by their size one must assume that the route was well patronised. At all events they are the handsomest things so far described in these pages, except for the ex-trolleybuses in Bilbao. A good-looking three-axle double-decker is nothing to sneeze at in these days; and the Viennese ones certainly don't look like single-deckers

An AEC looking rather the wrong way round, but otherwise relatively British; painted in the very smart yellow/white of the Coimbra Tramways.

with a growth on the top.

Even better-looking are the three-axle double-deckers in Turin. Like the Viennese vehicles, they are red and cream, but larger windows improve their appearance. Turin has also trolleybuses in various colours, and Visconti-type trams in Italian Ministry-of-Transport two-tone green, but all these are single-deckers. There is no doubt that a three-axle double-decker has a 'certain something'.

Other Italian double-deckers are not so admirable. Those in Naples and Rome have, for a start, only two axles; and besides this the front of the upper deck looks like the back of a Ford Anglia, and the back of the upper deck isn't there—that is to say it is cut away so that the roof slopes down at an angle of 45° to the level of the bottoms of the upper-deck windows. This decline indicates a fall in standards of Roman and Neapolitan bus design.

More conventional in design are German double-deckers; but Germany also boasts many examples of that rather rare bird the 1½-decker—so many in fact that it cannot be counted as rare in the Fatherland.

Berlin has a long tradition of double-deckers, having run double-deck trams in the days of Kaiser Wilhelm, and double-deck buses in the days of Hitler. In views of nasty Nazi parades jackbooting through Berlin one often sees a ferocious double-decker with an ugly snout in the background, behind the ugly snouts of the ferocious storm-troopers.

Similar machines, some of them three-axle, worked in Hamburg and on the Lübeck-Travemünde service. Hamburg had double-deck trolleybuses too, so it is said. But all Hamburg's double-deckers have disappeared; possibly to continue life on the other side of the Iron Curtain. In East Berlin there are still double-deck motor buses with snouts, but probably they are of post-Third Reich date. And the double-deckers now in West Berlin and on the Lübeck-Travemünde line are flat-fronted vehicles.

So are the rest of the West German double-deckers, for example in Mönchen-Gladbach, and, by contrast, on the rural services run by the Wurttembergische Eisenbahn. The buses of the latter concern run no doubt at the expense of its light railways.

These operators were among the first

followers of the present fashion for double-deckers in Germany; a fashion which presumably derived from 1½-deckers, which in their turn presumably came into existence when it became evident that the charming habit of bus trailers was going to be made illegal.

It is not perhaps entirely correct to discuss 1½-deckers in a treatise on double-deckers; but it may be argued that 1½-deckers are not single-deckers, and that their hinder quarters are double-deck, even if the lower deck is very claustrophobic. It would be rather unfair to leave them out. And all German 1½-deckers are, to their credit, on three axles.

Like the double-deckers of Germany, the 1½-deckers serve a wide range of territory; they may be found in the smoky townships of the Ruhrgebiet, in the timber-framed villages among the pretty hills, in the cowy-poplar-edged meadows of the plains. They work for anything from the thriving Cologne tramways to the rustic Westfälische Landes-Eisenbahn. They come also in trolleybus form, in Wuppertal, Hildesheim, and Osnabrück; as trolleybuses they look somewhat peculiar. As motorbuses they are not, for hybrid sort of things, ill-looking.

Above: A very British-looking double-deck Sunbeam trolleybus in an Oporto rainstorm.

Far left: A splendid Turin three-axle double-decker emerging from between statues of monumental proportions. One would have thought it hardly necessary to advertise Cinzano to the Italians.
Left: Children at play in the Champs de Mars, Paris, being watched by sightseers. Without the top deck this Saviem coach would be quite ordinary; with it, it is a Paris Vision.

A typical German double-decker with a typical German public service vehicle drink advertisement. This one belongs to the Wurttemburg local railways.

While speaking of Germany, a tentative mention of another Paris vision would, strangely enough, be in place; this because, although it was labelled as an inhabitant of Essen, it was wandering down the Rue Auber near the Opera, among the TN4H veterans. Because they were there I did not pay much attention to this nasty modern gleaming thing from Essen, but it was double-deck, and I believe it was on three axles. However, it was a sight-seeing bus, and it is only on proper service buses that three axles have any artistic merit. Besides, it was only a very fleeting vision I had of it, in a brief interval between red wine and boarding a TN to sightsee Paris the way God intended.

Besides this Essen vision, there are various two-axle double-decker sight-seeing coaches in Germany, and also in Holland and Sweden.

Scandinavia has certain traditions of double-deck operation, because there were double-deck tramcars in the early days in Copenhagen. In Stockholm today there are both British and German double-deck motor buses; the German examples are very like ordinary German double-deckers, and the British ones are very like ordinary British double-deckers, except for being rather huger and, of course, having left hand-drive and right-hand doors.

The Stockholm sight-seeing type is the ordinary sight-seeing type, of which no more need be said.

We observe from all this that double-decker buses are not entirely a British peculiarity; and further, that even if a number of double-deckers on the Continent are of British origin or design, none the less there are a number of native ones too; and even if some of the native ones tend to be outlandish, none the less those in Turin and Vienna may be reckoned preferable to most of the British models—which proves that foreigners can produce desirable double-deckers if they put their minds to it. So why do foreign students make such a racket when ascending the stairs of British buses?

Scottish fleetnames and colours

Buses Annual colour section

Western SMT¡ buses, like this Bristol/ ECW VRT (*below left*), carry a maroon/ cream livery, while coaches (*below*) are white/black.

Central SMT concentrates on urban operations, with buses like this Bristol Lodekka (*above*) and Bristol VRT (*right*), but there is a small fleet of Bedford coaches (*above right*).

65

When the Alexander empire was split into three, Alexanders (Fife) was given a red/cream livery, and Alexanders (Northern) a yellow/cream scheme. The photos show a Fife Tiger Cub and a Northern Albion Viking.

Alexanders (Midland) retained the old company blue/cream livery, and still uses the famous Bluebird symbol. The fleetname has been changed in recent years to the more modern style carried by this Daimler Fleetline in Falkirk.

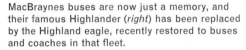

Scottish Omnibuses darkened its green livery some years ago and adopted the fleetname Eastern Scottish. A Bristol Lodekka (*left*) turns into Edinburgh's Princes Street; two AEC Reliance coaches wait at Edinburgh Castle (*below left*). To many the firm is still "SMT" and the old diamond (*top*) is its best-remembered symbol.

MacBraynes buses are now just a memory, and their famous Highlander (*right*) has been replaced by the Highland eagle, recently restored to buses and coaches in that fleet.

London Country oddities

Photographs by EDWARD SHIRRAS

Strictly there is nothing odd about London Country AEC Swift SM114 on route 426A, but it provides a useful link with the photos on the next three pages. The scene is Crawley (*National Bus Company photo*).

Right: One of the original batch of Merlins, MB96, conventional omo but two-door, seen at Hatfield on 303B—which amounts to one journey, one way only!

The Fleetlines at East Grinstead garage are generally confined to route 424, but very occasionally they stray to the 438 group. XF8 became a Blue Arrow at Stevenage.

The unique prototype Routemaster coach, RMC4, leaves Hatfield garage, where it is now used as a bus, mainly on 341/341B.

London Country AEC Swift Superbus at a Superbus stop in Stevenage en route from Chells to the bus station on the first day of operation, July 31, 1971.

Rosherville Gardens are now lost in an industrial area between Gravesend and Northfleet, by the Thames. Latterly this route was worked by omo RFs.

One of the AEC Swift/Willowbrook buses transferred to London Country from the South Wales fleet, at Shenley Hospital on 358.

The new invasion from Europe

GAVIN BOOTH examines wares in the Common Marketplace

There's nothing new about foreign buses in Britain. As Charles Klapper reminds us in his article elsewhere in this Annual, many of the earliest motor buses on British streets were foreign-made or at least foreign influenced. There was a resurgence of interest in overseas products just after World War I, when cheap lightweight coaches on pneumatic tyres were imported from the continent and the United States. These were fast and comfortable and had appeal at a time when the British manufacturers were still recovering from the War. As the British bus market developed and more sophisticated vehicles were evolved, fewer buses were bought from overseas, and throughout World War II right up to the late 1960s few, if any, British operators shopped abroad.

After World War II the British manufacturers were encouraged to become increasingly export-minded, to re-establish Britain in world markets, and, if anything, the home market suffered. Each of the big British builders, AEC, Daimler, Guy and Leyland, was associated with certain markets, but there was intense rivalry among them, particularly between AEC and Leyland. With Donald Stokes at the helm, Leyland enjoyed some spectacular successes in different parts of the world; the Commonwealth countries were always good markets, but there were good opportunities in war-torn Europe, particularly in those countries without a domestic bus-building industry. AEC and Leyland broke into the Dutch market with some success; Guy and Crossley enjoyed certain popularity in Belgium and Denmark. The outcome of these moves is that British Leyland now has strong subsidiary companies in three of the Northern European countries. Brossel in Belgium, Leyland-DAB in Denmark and Verheul in the Netherlands all assemble complete vehicles based on BLMC running units.

The big bus-producing countries are more difficult to penetrate. British Leyland psvs can be found in very limited quantities in France, but Germany and Italy, with highly-developed domestic builders, are not so easy.

On the home front, of course, British Leyland dominates the scene. As a group of islands, Britain was always able to pursue a very individualistic vehicle policy; now British vehicles are moving closer to their European counterparts. There are similarities too in the structure of the manufacturing industries. The trend has been towards the formation of bigger, stronger groups, by take-over or merger. British Leyland evolved this way by acquiring Standard-Triumph and Rover on the private car front, and AEC and British Motor Holdings (BMC and Jaguar) on the commercial front. Since the formation of British Leyland in 1968, the Corporation Truck and Bus Division has been rationalising the large psv range, which suffered badly from

Right: One of Leyland's recent successes in Europe was the sale of Panthers, like this one, and Atlanteans to Stockholm. All had Park Royal bodies.

Left: An example of the highly standardised DAF SB200 city bus, in service with the Utrecht undertaking.

model duplication. Now there are just seven companies within the Division producing full-size buses, AEC, Albion, Bristol, Daimler, Guy, Leyland and Leyland National; of these, Bristol and Leyland National are part-owned by the National Bus Company, and Albion and Guy are producing psvs mainly for export. This strong team—all deadly rivals less than 15 years ago—give British Leyland the dominant position it holds. In 1970 5,784 buses were built and 3,454 were exported. This secures BLMCs leading position in the domestic bus market, with competition from Seddon and the American-owned Bedford and Ford. Seddon has successfully re-established its position in the British market with its front and rear-engined Pennine chassis. Bedford and Ford have a

steady sale in the popular coach market, and have gained increasing popularity in the service bus field.

As Britain has slowly edged towards Europe, the British manufacturers have set their sights on the Common Market countries, but, more significantly, European builders have looked on Britain as a potential market.

The first rumblings came from Mercedes-Benz, the Teutonic giants who exhibited the highly refined 0302 model at the 1966 and 1968 London Commercial Shows. There were two problems as far as British operators were concerned, the difficulty of adapting the coach to suit the stringent regulations and the high purchase price. These problems were largely overcome and, though still expensive, Mercedes-Benz 0302 coaches have been placed in

Two Swedish examples of the Scania CR111.

service with a number of British operators.

Büssing—also from Germany—next entered the fray, and exhibited a Prafekt coach in the demonstration park at the 1968 London Show, and at the same time Moseley, the Loughborough dealers, showed the first Caetano coach body, Portuguese-built and marketed as Moseley Continental coachwork. Caetano bodies are now fairly common in Britain, and in 1970 the Belgian coachbuilder Van Hool exhibited at Earls Court for the first time—several British operators have now placed Van Hool-bodied coaches in service. The first Setra, like most German imports a complete coach, entered service in Britain in 1971, and Mercedes and Volvo are known to have strong interests in the British bus market, involving importing chassis only to receive bodies built to British regulations.

The first example of such co-operation is the Metro-Scania, a joint venture between Scania in Sweden and Metro-Cammell at Birmingham. The integral Metro-Scania single-decker is basically a British-built Metro-Cammell body, based on the Scania design, on Scania BR111 "chassis" imported from Sweden, and it may soon be joined by a double-deck version.

The race is on, and there can be little doubt that many unfamiliar makes will infiltrate British fleets in the near future. Before we examine the individual manufacturers who will challenge the British builders, it is useful to summarise the state of the bus business in each country.

First the six Common Market members.

A Büssing BS110V city bus in Wolfsburg, West Germany.

The bus-building industry in West Germany, as in most countries these days, is in the hands of a few powerful firms. The big five, Büssing, MAN, Magirus, Mercedes and Setra control a good part of the market, and each company offers a wide range of complete vehicles. The continentals, unlike British firms, usually offer complete bodied vehicles and strongly favour integral construction; in Britain only Leyland National and Seddon offer a complete one-firm vehicle, and only the National is integral.

The Germans have strong municipal pride, and there are 170 members in the VöV, the German municipal passenger transport association. All 170 banded together to fight out a standard specification for German city buses, and all the main manufacturers build models based on it.

Some 2,000 VöV buses can now be seen in service with municipal operators throughout Germany. The specification, originally fairly rigid, has been adapted to suit different needs as they arose.

Next door, the French municipal transport association has a standard bus specification of a more flexible nature and the two leading French manufacturers, Berliet (Citroen) and Saviem (Renault), produce virtually identical buses based on it. British Leyland's Belgian subsidiary, Brossel, also builds to this design for French municipalities. Otherwise Berliet and Saviem meet most of the demand, joined by an increasing number of imported coaches.

The Italian motor industry is dominated by Fiat, which produces large numbers of buses and coaches, as well as controlling Lancia and OM, two of the remaining psv builders. Fiat has a large export business, though in Northern Europe there are large numbers of Van Hool-assembled Fiat buses and coaches. Viberti, a large Italian bodybuilder, also assembles complete integral buses using Fiat and Lancia running units.

The remaining Common Market members are the Benelux countries. Tiny Luxembourg naturally allies with its neighbours Belgium and the Netherlands. Belgium has two well-known bus builders, Brossel, owned by British Leyland, and Van Hool, which com-

bines a large coachbuilding business with the assembly and sale of complete vehicles based on Fiat chassis. In the Netherlands DAF has emerged as an important force in the industry, where previously British firms had a major slice of the market. Certainly AEC and Leyland particularly are still much in evidence, partly through the British Leyland subsidiary Verheul which supplies complete vehicles based on BLMC chassis.

British Leyland has a large finger in the Northern European pie, with Verheul, Brossel and with DAB in Denmark, but there is strong competition for BLMC on the continent from "home" manufacturers, like Scania and Volvo. Although Sweden is not yet a Common Market country, these two firms are among the most active commercial vehicle exporters, and both are actively interested in the British bus business. These two firms have successfully penetrated the British truck scene, with over 20% of the heavy goods market between them, and Scania has indicated a target of 10,000 trucks in the UK by 1976.

The summary of the main European builders that starts on the next page provides background information on the Common Market manufacturers and other major continental bus and coach builders who have set their sights on the British market. These are the principal names. There are others—smaller chassis builders and coachbuilders who also construct complete vehicles using proprietary components.

The situation is an interesting one. For the first time for many years the continentals have gained a foothold in Britain, and this invasion, mostly from Germany and the Scandanavian countries. The British manufacturers are ready for this onslaught, and the Common Market will give them fresh opportunities to break into Europe. Lord Stokes, Chairman of British Leyland, has stated his aims: "By 1975 the company plan to sell 500,000 vehicles a year on the continent, which is more than double the number they sold there in 1970." Just as our new European neighbours mean business, so does Lord Stokes.

Büssing BS110V city bus.

The lion of Brunswick is also the symbol of the Büssing company, one of the best known German bus builders. Heinrich Büssing started building buses in 1904, and in 1907 built Berlin's first double-deck bus—now there are more than 1,000 double-deckers on the streets of West Berlin. Büssing double-deckers can also be seen in the service of other German municipal operators, and in Stockholm and Vienna.

Büssing is probably best known as a bus builder, but the firm also produces trucks, trolleybuses and engines for railcars. To meet demands for increased passenger space, Büssing pioneered the underfloor-engined layout for buses in 1934, and two years later such vehicles were in full production.

Although more than half the buses operated by German municipal operators are Büssings, the firm negotiated with MAN in 1969, resulting in MAN buying a 50% stake in Bussing.

The current range covers buses, coaches, articulated buses, $1\frac{1}{2}$-deck buses and double-deckers, with underfloor or rear engines. Büssing exhibited a Prafekt coach at the 1968 Commercial Show in London, and a Yorkshire firm has set up an agency to import right hand drive Büssings.

MAN 750 U12 touring coach.

M·A·N Maschinenfabrik Augsburg-Nurnberg AG, the German firm better known as MAN, claims to be the oldest builders of diesel engines—successful tests were carried out in 1897. In 1955 the firm transferred to Munich from Nurnberg, where it had started. Now a full range of commercials is built, with French partner Saviem designing and building smaller goods vehicles, marketed as MANs. There are also strong links within the German industry, for in 1969 MAN bought a 50% stake in Büssing.

At present the psv range is based on a small number of models, available with a wide range of body styles and sizes. The basic models are the 535HO and 750HO models, the designations identifying the engines used. There is also a larger engine, used mainly in the 890UG articulated models.

Like Mercedes, MAN is involved in a full programme of research and experiment. The firm is working on "genuine" electric buses, a bus propelled by liquefied natural gas, and on gas turbine trucks.

Magirus 120 R80 coach.

MAGIRUS DEUTZ

Magirus Deutz buses are made by another old-established German firm. The manufacturers which make up the present-day Klöckner-Humboldt-Deutz AG empire date back to the nineteenth century, but Magirus, the firm most concerned with passenger vehicles, built its first bus in 1919, and still offers a wide range of buses and coaches.

In common with other German manufacturers, the Magirus range of complete vehicles covers small, medium and long buses and coaches, and these are available with a choice of engines and seating arrangements.

Mercedes-Benz 0317 city bus.

Biggest and best known of the German manufacturers, Daimler-Benz AG results from the fusion in 1926 of the separate businesses of Karl Benz and Gottlieb Daimler, both founded in the nineteenth century. The Mercedes name was adopted at the time of the merger. Mercedes delivers 700 buses per week, and the giant Mannheim plant churns out 200 complete buses and 250 bus chassis each week. Of the complete vehicles, 35% are exported; of the chassis, 80% are exported.

The present range covers forward, underfloor and rear-engined designs in a variety of sizes. The rear-engined 0302 coach is a familiar sight throughout the world—even in Britain as Mercedes was one of the first continental manufacturers to infiltrate the British market. The Daimler-Benz version of the German VöV standard city bus is the 0305, and it seems possible that we may see British-bodied versions in service. Well over 1,000 0305s are in service in Germany. The longer-established 0317 bus has an underfloor engine, and has been used as the basis for single-deck, 1½-deck, double-deck and articulated buses.

Setra S80 touring coach.

Setra is a contraction of the German word **Selbsttra**gend, meaning self-supporting—in other words, integrally built. Coachbuilder Karl Kassbohrer first built vehicles in 1893, and in 1911 bodied his first bus. The first complete integral Setra was built in 1951, and now a wide range of complete passenger vehicles is constructed at Ulm, in addition to the truck bodies, trailers and tankers that are still built for other chassis.

The psv range is based on the rear-engined S model, offered as S80, S110, S120, S130 and S150—progressively larger from 7·69 m to 12 m, and identified by the number of rows of seats; hence the S80, with eight rows of seats, is basically a 34-seater. Lower built and flat-floor models are available for special needs. The S125 model (up to 125 passengers) is a city bus, and the SG175 is an articulated model. Setra's VöV bus is the S130S. Other special types can be built to order, and the company has built apron buses for airports, and luxurious 1½-deck coaches based on the S150. One Setra coach, an S130, entered service with an Essex operator in late 1971.

Imported Bedford VAL/Van Hool.

Van Hool, the Belgian coachbuilding firm, should not strictly be included in this survey, but as a leading exporter from a Common Market country which has sold bus bodies to Britain, and as a builder of complete vehicles based on Fiat running units, it merits attention.

The firm started building bus bodies in 1947, and ten years later entered an arrangement with Fiat to build complete buses and coaches. This has enabled Van Hool to offer a wide selection of vehicles specially tailored to suit the North European market. Of the 1,200 buses produced each year, some 60% is exported to all parts of the world. In France, for example, Van Hool is the main importer of buses. Van Hool claims to cover 70% of the Benelux market.

In addition to the Fiat-based range, Van Hool bodies are built on other chassis, and Bedford and Leyland coaches have been supplied to British operators.

Van Doorne's Automobielfabrieken, DAF, based in Eindhoven in the Netherlands, was founded in 1928 to build trailers for lorries. Commercial vehicles were built from 1950, and the popular DAF car dates back only to 1958.

DAF exports 42% of its commercial vehicles, and the firm supplies 67% of the Dutch bus market. Leyland had a strong stake in the Netherlands in the postwar years, and early DAF buses had engines based on Leyland units. Now the DAF SB200 is the mainstay of the Dutch municipal market. This, the most standard of standard buses, was evolved by the local undertakings at Amsterdam, Rotterdam, The Hague and Utrecht. Over 500 have been supplied to these four municipalities since 1967, and it is estimated that these fleets will contain only SB200s by 1980.

In recent years DAF has enjoyed a spectacular success in the heavy commercial market, and the bus range is being extended to meet the demands of the new export markets.

DAF MB200 with coach body.

berliet

Like the French car industry, the French commercial vehicle industry is mainly in the hands of two giants, and although they sell under different names, they are the same two giants. Saviem is part of the government-owned Renault empire; Berliet merged with Citroen in 1967. Marcus Berliet built his first engine in 1894, his first car in 1898. From 1906 he made commercials, and from 1930 diesel engines.

The firm decided to concentrate on heavy vehicles in 1939, and now Berliet claims to be the largest Common Market producer of commercial vehicles—30,000 a year, 2,000 of which are buses, mainly for France and French-influenced countries.

Through its connections with Citroen, Berliet has links with Fiat, Autobianchi and Maserati.

The Berliet range contains small, medium and large chassis and complete vehicles. The PH range features underfloor engines, the Cruisair coach range is rear-engined and the PCM is the Berliet version of the standard French city bus, with engine under the driving position. A shorter version of the PCM, the PGR, is also available.

Berliet Cruisair PR3A coach.

SAVIEM

The Societe Anonyme de Véhicules Industriels et d'Equipements Mécaniques—Saviem—is a recent arrival on the French commercial vehicle scene. It was formed in 1955 when Renault and Latil merged, and in 1956 Floirat and Isobloc were acquired. In 1959 Saviem merged with Chausson, one of the largest French bus builders, to become one of the major forces on the market.

Saviem has an arrangement with Alfa-Romeo, which produces goods vehicles to Saviem design, and associated in 1967 with the German firm MAN.

Saviem functions as Renault's heavy commercial vehicle division, sharing the bulk of the French market with Berliet.

The range is comprehensive, containing all sizes of buses and coaches in chassis form and as complete vehicles. The S range features underfloor engines of MAN and Saviem design; the SC range is front-engined, vertically-mounted on the SC5 and SC6, under the driving position on the SC10 city bus, the near twin of the Berliet PCM. These two near-identical models can be seen on the streets of most French towns—well over 1,500 of the Saviem SC10 are in service.

Saviem SC10 standard city bus.

Fiat 343 touring coach.

Fiat, Fabbrica Italiana Automobili Torino, was founded in Italy in 1899. It has grown rapidly to become the immense industrial organisation of today, employing 185,000, and producing almost every type of transport vehicle from small cars to reactors for nuclear ships, diesel and electric locomotives and complete jet aircraft. Fiat has agreements with Citroen and Ferrari, and owns two well-known Italian bus builders, Lancia and OM.

The Fiat commercial vehicle range is very comprehensive, and the psv models cover all types of buses and coaches. After clinging to forward-engined buses for some time, the Italians are following the European trend and favour underfloor and rear engines for full-size vehicles. The 306 and 308 inter-city buses, and 410A and 418AL city buses all have underfloor engines. The 343 coach and small 416A bus have rear engines, and the small (6.35m) 625 has a forward engine. The recently-introduced 421A city bus has the engine mounted under the driving position, French style. Indeed the 421A is similar in concept to many of the standard city buses elsewhere in Europe today, and has strong similarities to the German VöV designs and the French Berliet and Saviem buses.

Scania CR145 luxury coach.

SCANIA

Scania-Bussar AB of Katrineholm, Sweden, was formed in 1967 to handle the increased demand for new buses when Sweden changed over to right-hand traffic.

The origins of the firm really date to 1911 when two separate engineering firms Scania and Vabis merged, and the firm pioneered many types of bus, mainly designed to suit Scandinavian conditions. In fact, bus manufacture was the largest part of Scania Vabis activity for many years.

Complete vehicles and bare chassis are built, differentiated by their type prefixes, BR for chassis and CR for complete vehicles. The BR110, for instance, is the basis of the British-assembled Metro-Scania.

Scania trucks have become increasingly common on British roads, and by the end of 1971 some 2,500 were in service. The Metro-Scania single-deck bus has enjoyed healthy sales since it first appeared in production form in 1970, and a double-deck version is in preparation.

Volvo B58 city bus in Athens.

AB Volvo first experimented with cars in Sweden in 1926, and the first production models were built in 1927. Now Volvo is Scandanavia's largest engineering industry, responsible for more than 7% of Sweden's total exports—it is, in fact, the largest exporter in the country.

Volvo and Scania have had considerable success supplying heavy goods vehicles to Britain, and, like Scania, Volvo has firm designs on the British bus market. Two chassis will support their plans, the underfloor-engined B58 and the rear-engined B59 city bus chassis. Already the B59 has been chosen by Copenhagen municipality, and it could well be a popular choice for Britain.

Volvo build chassis only, unusual for a continental manufacturer, and the current range, in addition to the B58 and B59, includes the front-engined B57, best suited to Scandanavian conditions.

Museum pieces/1: the Castleruddery Museum

MICHAEL CORCORAN
describes an ambitious project

A cheerful aspect of the transport scene nowadays is a growing interest in preservation and if the efforts of those working in this field are permanently successful posterity certainly will not be unhappy about its heritage. Great Britain is much favoured in this respect and an enthusiast living outside the United Kingdom, like the present writer, can only marvel at the achievements of the conservationists and envy them the advantages conferred by a huge population and an almost unlimited choice of vehicles.

In Ireland the position is somewhat different but nevertheless interesting. To make comparisons, however, one must consider Ireland's population of only 4.5 m. of whom about 3 m. live in the Republic of Ireland, as well as the fact that the number of buses in the whole island is less than 5,000. It must also be borne in mind that preoccupation with other matters because of a troubled history and until recently, a lower standard of living, have produced conditions unlike those in Britain. Yet progress has been made and while some of us have been impatient with its pace the story is not disheartening and some of the methods and procedures used may commend themselves to our colleagues in the United Kingdom.

Preservation in the Republic of Ireland began in 1949 when a small band of enthusiasts bought three Dublin trams but these eventually succumbed to vandalism, although recent developments have ensured that at least one car from this renowned system will be seen again. Such bitter experience, coupled with a general apathy towards preservation and the relatively small number of enthusiasts, put transport conservation squarely in

A The lane leading to the museum, with ex-London trolleybus 1348 stuck in the gateway, in May 1970.

81

the doldrums until 1968 when a number of important developments occurred.

Despite their troubles, the Transport Museum Society managed to preserve a few vehicles, including three psvs which Coras Iompair Eireann generously stored in their garages until a suitable home could be found for them. These were DUTC R1 (ZC 714), a Leyland Titan TD4 of 1937 with Leyland H58R body; Leyland K2 trolleybus EXV 348 of 1939 given by London Transport in whose fleet it was 1348; and GNR Gardner 390 (IY 7384) of 1952 with GNR/PRV DP33R body which, like R1, was given by CIE, whose attitude to preservation has been consistently most helpful.

More vehicles were offered to the Society in 1968 and it was clear that a make-or-break situation then existed. Painful examination of the collective conscience took place and it was decided to seek outside help. An approach was therefore made to the then Minister for Finance who happened to represent the writer's constituency in the Dail and who was known to be sympathetic to voluntary organisations endeavouring to improve the quality of life in Ireland. The Minister gave advice and from that moment things began to go right.

The Society was reorganised and steps were taken to have register it as a limited company; a site was sought and public assistance solicited from the Tourist Board (Bord Failte). Through the help of the West Wicklow Development Association, a field of 3.766 acres was located at Castleruddery, Donard in the Glen of Imaal and this was bought for £600. It is 35 miles from Dublin and in an area which will eventually form part of a vast national park. Plans were quickly prepared and planning permission obtained for a building measuring 150 ft by 40 ft, with as big a future extension. The tourist authorities agreed to make a grant of £2,000 and this was later matched by a similar allocation from Wicklow County Council, the project being costed at around £8,000.

Meanwhile further vehicles were acquired, and here it is noteworthy that many public authorities and firms in Ireland make rolling stock available to the Society on a permanent loan basis, preservation agreements being signed in each case. Several interesting units were taken into stock, including fire engines, military types, municipal vehicles and general transport as well as more PSVs.

B 1939 ex-London K2 trolleybus 1348 at Castleruddery.

C ZI 9708, the ex-DUT 1933 Dennis Lancet 32-seater.

82

Among the latter were: AEC Regent III ZH 3937, which has Park Royal H56RD bodywork and was 438 in the GNR fleet; Belfast Corporation Guy BTX trolleybus 183 (GZ 8547) of 1949 with Harkness H68R bodywork; and a purchased vehicle which is a rare find these days; ZI 9708, a 1933 Dennis Lancet with DUTC B32R body which had originally been F21 in the Dublin fleet. Although woebegone when bought it is eminently restorable. With it was obtained ZI 1728, a Leyland TS1 Tiger of 1931 but this was irreparably damaged by vandals before it could be removed.

Building work began in December 1969 and was slow, ready cash being the biggest problem. Structurally, the building consists of ten haybarn type spans of 40 ft by 15 ft with round truss roof and panel concrete block walls between the stanchions and piers on the outside; toilets and a small souvenir shop and office block are incorporated. By May 1970 work was well advanced and on the 17th of that month we were honoured to have as our first guests on the site members of the Omnibus Society then visiting Ireland.

As well as native types, it is hoped to exhibit outstanding vehicle designs from other areas and to this end the Society bought Sunbeam trolleybus 299 from Bournemouth Corporation, which it is hoped will be joined by other expatriates. Irish vehicles obtained during 1970 were GZ 7638, a 1947 Leyland Tiger PS1 with NIRTB B34R body (Fleet No. A8570) and MZ 7396, ex-Belfast 298, a Guy Arab/Harkness B32F given by OS Coaches of Hospital, Co. Limerick.

Castleruddery was inaugurated officially with a fete in July 1971 and thereafter work was concentrated on completing and fitting out the building. At the time of writing in December 1971 a grounds layout had been prepared and it is expected that the official opening will take place in the spring of 1972, with about 16 restored vehicles on show: the total stock is at present 30 vehicles, some of which are at present undergoing renovation. Among these is former Hill of Howth Tramway Car 9, which was the last tram to run in Ireland.

A very interesting former psv was obtained from CIE in 1971. It is a Leyland Lion LT2 lorry GT6 (AZ 5078) which began its career as GNR bus 110 in 1931 and it will be joined later by yet another GNR vehicle; Garage Tender No. 2, a prewar Gardner complete with workshop

D IY 7384, the 1952 GNR Gardner which is one of the main exhibits.

body and gantry. One of 1971's important developments was the submission to CIE of a list of PSVs worthy of preservation and due for withdrawal over the next five years: hopefully all nine vehicles will eventually sojourn to Castleruddery.

While the scale of our operations is small compared to those in the United Kingdom, we take great pride in the Castleruddery museum. But we have also learned some hard lessons, above all that at our stage of development we must not get complacent, we must keep up the momentum and we must plan ahead. Three rules I heartily commend to all conservationists. Our paramount consideration is that today's common-place vehicle will be tomorrow's museum piece; history is a continuing process of which we are all part and our heritage of preserved vehicles reflect our national, transport and social history in a unique way. Yet when all is said and done, our greatest pleasure is to share our transport treasures with others and British enthusiasts, who have helped and advised us in countless ways, will always find a ready and sincere welcome at Castleruddery.

Variety in standardisation—
London's STL class

ALAN TOWNSIN MIMechE probes the complexities

The STL class is generally remembered as London Transport's first big move towards bus standardisation. The class was LT's largest until overtaken in size by the postwar RT programme. And, of the 2,679 STL buses, over 2,000 were of the same outline and had basically the same mechanical specification.

But when examined more closely, the STL class was surprisingly complex. Over 80 variations were indicated by the London Transport chassis and body code system—it is almost impossible to give an exact figure, for some combinations only existed temporarily as a result of body transfers. Indeed quite a number of the variations were caused by abnormal transfers of bodies on to chassis they were not intended for, due to the war. But even ignoring abnormalities of this kind, and minor variations, there were about 16 major types.

The origin of the STL class can be traced directly to the new range of buses introduced

by London Transport's principal bus-operating predecessor, the London General Omnibus Co. Ltd., in 1929–30. So far as double-deckers were concerned, these consisted of the two-axle AEC Regent, model 661, with its original wheelbase of 15 ft 6½ in., generally with 49-seat body, which the LGOC designated ST, and the three-axle AEC Renown, model 663, seating 56 or 60, which was designated LT. From a designation viewpoint, these classes were respectively short and long

variations of the T class, which was the single-deck AEC Regal, model 662. This was an illogical arrangement, for the T class was soon outnumbered by both ST and LT classes. The AEC concern was, in those days, a subsidiary of LGOC.

The LGOC put large fleets of both ST and LT buses on the road, the STs mainly in 1930 and most of the LTs during 1931–32. Three-axle buses had been in fashion in the 1920s, but by 1932 new vehicles of this type

were quite rare in Britain outside London. Changes in legislation had made it possible to put 26 ft-long two-axle double-deckers on the road instead of the previous maximum of 25 ft. The LT-class double-deckers measured 26ft 9in.

So AECs new longer version of the Regent, with 16 ft 3 in wheelbase, was introduced early in 1932. The LGOC was by no means the first to put examples into service, even in London, as will emerge later. But its aim was ambitious —to produce a two-axle bus capable of carrying the same number of seated passengers, 60, as the later LT models. Few other operators had gone beyond about 52 seats, even on the newly-introduced 26 ft double-deckers. It was decided to call this lengthened ST the STL.

The styles of bodywork built in its own Chiswick works by the LGOC at the time were decidedly square-cut. It was only necessary to push the upper-deck front win-

dows a few inches further forward, almost to the limit of the roof, to allow 34 seats to be fitted on the top deck—I believe this was the highest upper-deck capacity on any British two-axle double-decker until after World War II. This meant that the lower-deck capacity had to be 26, higher than average at the time, but not difficult.

The gross weight limit applying at that time was 10 tons and this implied paring some weight off, as compared to the standard ST, despite the new vehicle's larger size. Particular attention had to be paid to the upper deck in view of the tilt test requirements. When the first bus, STL1, was introduced in January 1933, the unladen weight was 5 tons 18 cwt, a remarkably low figure.

This was firstly achieved by adoption of a fairly simple mechanical specification. The LGOC had been a pioneer in the adoption of the diesel engine—in those days generally called simply the oil engine—for buses. The

same applied to the combination of fluid flywheel and preselective epicyclic gearbox. Out of 1072 LT double-deckers built in 1931–32, 105 had oil engines, 54 had preselective gearboxes plus a further 20 which had both. Results were promising, but of the 100 60-seat STL buses built, none were diesel and only one had a preselective gearbox. The engine used was basically the same six-cylinder overhead-camshaft unit as used on the ST, with 100 mm by 130 mm bore and stroke, giving a swept volume of 6·1 litres. Power output depended on carburetter and other variables but was generally about 95 bhp. Most long-wheelbase Regents sold to operators outside London at the time were of the 110 mm bore (7·4 litre) type developing between 110 and 120 bhp.

Transmission on all but one was by clutch and four-speed "crash" gearbox. The unit used was the AEC D124, with sliding-mesh first and second and constant-mesh third

gear. Brakes were of vacuum-hydraulic type, a newly introduced option at the time and one which was to be found on most STLs.

The 60-seaters were numbered STL 1–50 and STL 153–202. In sorting out the variations of the class it is helpful to refer to the coding system used by London Transport, with prefix numbers for chassis variants and suffix numbers for body variants. Thus STL 1–49 had chassis of type 1 STL and STL 1 bodies, making the complete vehicle code 1 STL 1. STL 50 was the bus with preselective gearbox —a Daimler-made unit, classified D128 by AEC with pedestal-type gear selector unit looking rather like a miniature ship's engine-room telegraph. This was chassis code 3 STL and the different floor trap openings made the body STL 1/1. The second batch of standard 60-seaters, STL 153–202, were 2 STL 1, having a different chassis code because of a different exhaust system. Curiously, variations of rear axle type on these early buses were not coded, probably because they did not affect interchangeability.

Part of the gap between the first and second batches of 60-seaters was filled with 80 buses which were built for Thomas Tilling Ltd. The London Passenger Transport Board came into official existence on July 1, 1933, taking over the LGOC on that date and most other operators in London in fairly quick succession. The official take-over of Tilling's London business was not until October 1, 1933, but co-operation began earlier. So Tilling's long-wheelbase Regents took numbers in the LGOC series during the four months before the LPTB took over. The first had appeared before LGOCs own examples, in November 1932, and the number ST 837 was originally allocated (this was later used for the first of Tilling's older open-staircase Regents to be taken over) but the batch became STL 51–130.

The chassis were basically similar to those of STL 1–49, though having numerous minor differences. LGOC/LPTB Regents almost always differed from the standard models as supplied to other operators and the Tilling buses were nearer to AECs 1932–3 standard in such respects as mudguard design, though having quite a few Tillingisms. It is possible that, originally, they had 95 mm bore versions of the AEC engine, with swept volume of only 5·5 litres (A 137). The bodies, built by Tilling's, were quite different. They were less angular, seated 56 and although having some ungainly detail work (three forward-facing windows at the front of the upper deck, for example) had modern touches in the more rounded outline and tubular steel seat frames. Some 22 buses for which fleet numbers STL 131–152 had been allocated were never built and these numbers were never used. The Tilling STLs were not at first given codes, but later became 8 STL 4.

More by coincidence than otherwise, the formation of the LPTB was almost immediately followed by the apperance of a new, more modern-looking style of bodywork from Chiswick Works, although this had been planned by the LGOC. Seating capacity was 56, with 30 on the top deck, and this was to remain the standard for almost all later STLs. A more sloping body front profile was adopted, and the rear was more curved, though the Y-shaped centre pillar to the emergency exit was to remain as a characteristic feature of almost all STLs. The first 50 buses, STL 203–252, ordered by LGOC, were based on preselective gearbox chassis as STL 50. The unladen weight was 5 tons 18 cwt. They had 110 mm engines, and were classified 3 STL 2 and 1/3 STL 2, the latter, of which there were 25, having a modified cylinder head.

The next 350 buses, delivered in 1933–34 and the first to be ordered by LPTB were outwardly similar, except that the front upper-deck windows were flush with the front panels, instead of being slightly recessed and set in a V-formation. But all except 11 of them were concerned in an unusual engine-swap exercise. They received 110 mm bore petrol engines from LT class buses which were being converted to diesel. Part of the reasoning behind this was no doubt to get the greater fuel cost savings from the heavier buses. But another factor may have been that the 8·8-litre A165 oil engines were about 4½ in longer than the petrol units. As the STLs were of maximum legal length, shorter bodies would have had to be fitted. This was accepted on many Regents built for other operators at the time, but interchangeability of bodies was important to London Transport, when bodies were removed and normally refitted to other chassis every couple of years or so in the course of overhaul. Body repairs took longer than chassis so about 103 bodies were built for every 100 chassis at that time.

Besides, AEC had a new oil engine which fitted in the same space as the petrol engine and the 11 chassis mentioned were among the first 12 to be so fitted (the other was a conversion of LT 21). This was the A171 engine, of, originally, 106 mm bore and 146 mm stroke, giving a swept volume of 7.7 litres. Later the bore was reduced to 105 mm, making the swept volume 7·58 litres, though the engine was generally still called the 7.7.

STL 253–291 had D128 preselector gear-boxes with selector levers looking like con-

The sloping-front STL, as represented by STL 420, photographed in postwar days. This was one of the 286 buses with preselective gearboxes, converted from petrol to diesel in 1939—in this case altering from 7 STL 3/2 code to 2/16 STL 18. The bus shown was one of the few of this type repainted green during or after the War.

ventional gear levers and were apparently classified 4 STL 3/2. The eleven oil-engined buses were STL 342–352 and they had the same transmission, being classified 5 STL 3/1 (the body differed in electrical equipment, etc. to suit the diesel chassis). STL 292–341 and 353–402 had crash gear boxes and were 6 STL 3. STL 403–552 and STL 559–608 were more preselector buses, but these had the newly introduced AEC-made gear box, type D132, and were 7 STL chassis, the bodies being as STL 253–291. Records exist of STL 3/3 and 3/4 bodies built in 1933, but the differences are not known.

The gap STL 553–558 in these numbers was filled by long-wheelbase Regents taken over from independent operators, all built in the spring and early summer of 1932 and thus slightly older than any other STLs. Five buses came from C. H. Pickup, an aptly-named proprietor based in Dulwich, and were notable as being the first "modern" open-toppers, built thus from choice after covered

tops had become standard in the mid-1920s. They had Park Royal bodies, well up to contemporary up-to-date standards, with enclosed staircases. But London Transport was not impressed with the idea, and built STL 3-type top decks for them at Chiswick. They married up quite well, except that there were five windows upstairs against six below. They were subsequently classified 12 STL 8 for STL 553–556, which had vacuum-mechanical brakes and 1/12 STL 8 for STL 557 which had vacuum-hydraulic.

STL 558 was, if anything, even more odd. Built for Red Line (E. Brickwood Ltd.) of London, W10, it had an up-to-date chassis,

Top: The standard STL outline was evolved by August 1934 with the introduction of the 9 STL 5 type. STL 690 would probably be mistaken for a current London bus by many bystanders today. *Above:* The 12 special Weymann-bodied low-height STLs built in 1934 for operation from Godstone garage had little in common with other LT buses, other than the chassis. They were coded 11 STL 7. The last of the batch, STL 1055, was photographed at Staines shortly before withdrawal.

with D128 preselective gearbox, but a decidedly old-fashioned-looking body built by Birch Bros. to typical London independent style. It did, however, have an enclosed staircase, uncommon on this style of body, but ironically it suffered a rear-end collision in 1934 and received the rear-end of a similar but open-staircase body from an ex-independent Daimler. It was coded 13 STL 9, and was the first of the class to be withdrawn from service (in 1946) apart from the 61 buses (mostly dating from 1933–34) destroyed in the war.

The next production STL buses set the pattern for three-quarters of the whole class. STL 609–758 had A 171 oil engines, as on STL 342–352, but with AEC-made D132 preselective gearbox. The bodywork, although structurally similar to previous ash-framed products from Chiswick works, set new standards for appearance—indeed, it was a trend-setter for British double-deckers generally. The main novelty was the adoption of a smoothly curved profile from cab front panel to roof, a feature later to be widely copied, but novel on a half-cab motor bus in August 1934. Another change from previous LGOC/LPTB practice was the gentle curve of the lower edge of the driver's windscreen and the lower-deck front bulkhead windows. The latter was arranged to be only a couple of inches above the bonnet level, giving much better vision from the front passenger seats than on most double-deckers.

London Transport was just beginning to establish its reputation for high standards of visual design. Apart from the external appearance, the interior made imaginative use of colour, with the trim over the lower half of the pillars and waistrail coloured brown and the upper half and cantrail light green. But the seats continued to be the low-backed wood-framed type first introduced in 1932. These buses were classified 9 STL 5, and 200 more buses of basically similar design followed, STL 759–958, most of which were classified 1/9 STL 5/1. Although the production of STL buses was in progress on a large scale during the 1935–39 period, minor changes in design were introduced from time to time and some of these were not indicated by the codes. Rubber engine mountings (not the true flexible engine mounting which came later) appeared to have come in part-way through the 1/9 STL chassis.

An odd man out was STL 857, with fully-fronted body incorporating a grille hiding the normal chassis radiator. This appeared towards the end of 1935 and was temporarily renumbered STF 1 a few months later, but was rebuilt with conventional half cab and exposed radiator in 1938. But although the full-front idea was dropped, other features of the body were later adopted as standard. These included a new design of polished aluminium tubular-framed seats with double top rails that set the pattern for London bus seats ever since and, even in original form, were far more comfortable than many present-day seats.

These seats were incorporated in the last 20 bodies for the STL 759–958 batch of buses, these bodies being classified STL 5/2. Meanwhile, a batch of what would nowadays generally be called forward-entrance bodies (front-entrance was the usual term at the time) were built for the country area in the winter of 1934–5. An attempt was made to avoid draughts without using doors by angling the bulkhead, and the space over the rear wheel arches was used for luggage instead of seats, reducing the seating capacity to 48 (29 up, 19 down). Most were given four more seats downstairs in 1939. In detail design these buses resembled the 9 STL 5, apart from the entrance and consequential differences; they were classified 10 STL 6. The main batch of 85 buses were STL 959–1043, but a further four, STL 1056–1059, followed in the summer of 1935. So small a number of buses in a batch was unusual for LT.

The gap STL 1044–1055 was filled by 12 buses ordered by London General Country Services Ltd. The chassis numbers, issued by AEC at the date of ordering, were earlier than those of the STL 153 upwards batch, but the buses were not delivered until the spring of 1934. Even then they were not given STL fleet numbers, which were not used until the Reigate-based country department handed over responsibility for vehicle matters to 55 Broadway, SW1, in 1935.

These vehicles were built primarily for use from Godstone garage on the route to Reigate which in those days passed under a low bridge. They were accordingly of side-gangway low-height type. They were also of front-entrance layout, helping to set a temporary fashion for such vehicles (followed by STL 959, etc. among others). Apart from being based on 16 ft 3 in wheelbase Regent chassis, they had virtually nothing in common with any other STL models. The engines were A165 8·8-litre diesels, at the time the standard AEC oil engine, but the only examples in an STL. Gearboxes were standard D124 "crash" units. The 48-seat bodywork, built by Weymann, was of this builder's standard style of the period, as supplied to company and

Windy corner. The forward-entrance STLs built for country service in 1935 and 1936 had no doors and the entrance layout was designed, not too successfully, to reduce draughts. This is STL 1513, the last bus of the second batch, with Weymann-built body to Chiswick specification, coded 1/10 STL 6/1.

municipal operators in other parts of the country. Almost the only external Londonism was the extensive destination blind equipment. They were coded 11 STL 7.

STL 1060–1259 were another 200 standard STLs, classified 2/9 STL 11, the chassis incorporating slight modifications to the preselective gearbox. The bodies were, in effect, a slightly improved version of the STL 5/2, double-panelled throughout and with modified indication layout, with destination box above rather than below route and number boxes. This feature had appeared on STL 857/STF 1 and although this body had a more sloping front of the upper deck, it was coded STL 11 —latterly it was transferred to STL 1167.

The normally consistent and orderly policy of London Transport sometimes seemed to hiccough and so it was with STL 1260–1263. The LGOC had bought three Daimler CH6 double-deckers in 1930 to gain experience of the then new preselective transmission, soon adopted as standard for London buses. Another CH 6 double-decker came from the Redline concern, original owners of STL 558. In 1936 it was decided to sell the CH 6 chassis, non-standard to LT and fitted with sleeve-valve petrol engines which suffered from heavy lubricating oil consumption. The surprising thing was the decision to fit the bodies, then decidedly dated in style and six years old (body life was often no more than eight years in those days), to brand new chassis. Moreover the standard STL chassis would not fit and special shorter chassis had to be made, though of up-to-date diesel and preselective specification.

Thus STL 1260/1 and 3 had LGOC bodies outwardly like those of the ST class and seating 48 while STL 1262 had a Dodson 52-seat body from the ex-Redline bus. All were classified 14 STL 10. STL 1262 actually received an ex-LGOC ST class body when the Dodson body was scrapped in 1944 and was rebuilt to normal length and fitted with a standard STL body in 1947.

Order was restored with STL 1264–1463 and 1514–1613, 300 buses generally classified 3/9 STL 11, again with minor chassis modifications but the same body as STL 1060–1259.

A batch of 50 more front-entrance buses for the country area were STL 1464–1513, built in 1936, and classified 1/10 STL 6/1. These were almost identical to STL 959, etc in general appearance, but had metal-framed bodywork built by Weymann. The styling followed the Chiswick pattern quite closely, though slightly more pronounced radii at the top of the upper deck front windows gave a characteristic clue to their origin. Seats and other body details followed the STL 11 pattern, though the total seating capacity remained at 48.

Then followed no less than 902 rear-entrance buses with 4/9 STL chassis, numbered STL 1614–2515. The chassis differed only in detail from other variations of the 9 STL, still with indirect injection. Most of the first 400, numbered STL 1614–2013 and built in 1936–37, had bodies generally similar to the STL 11 but with roof-mounted roof number box, a revival of 1931–32 practice, coded STL 14. The actual change-over point from STL 11 to STL 14 body did not coincide with STL 1614, even when new —chassis and fleet numbers were kept in strict order, which did not necessarily tie up with the order of arrival of chassis at Chiswick. Unladen weight had by this time settled down at 6 tons 12 cwt.

Forty buses out of this batch, with numbers between STL 1809 and 1884, had a special version of Chiswick-built body designed to operate through the Blackwall and Rotherhithe tunnels. They had more arched roofs than standard, more raked upper-deck front ends and a modified staircase reducing the lower deck seating capacity by one, making the total 55. They were classified STL 13 and were built in 1937.

The batch STL 2014–2188 had bodies built by Park Royal outwardly to standard roof-number-box STL design but with welded metal-framed construction of the bodybuilder's own pattern. Internally, these 175 bodies were easily identified by the semicircular pillar trim section, introducing an appearance later to become familiar in less extreme form in the RT-type body. These vehicles were also built in 1937, the bodies being classified STL 15.

STL 2189–2415 had Chiswick-built bodies classified STL 14/1 and STL 2416–2515 had almost identical STL 12 bodies, the differences being mainly in the construction of the wheel-arches. The STL 12, 14 and 14/1 bodies were almost identical and the combined total of 687 buses originally fitted with them could be counted as the largest group of similar buses in the whole STL class. There were variations, however, and the last three buses, STL 2513–5, at first had 8·8 litre engines, presumably of similar type to those in the 10T10 Green Line single-deck coaches built about the same time, 1938, with direct injection. They were evidently only intended as a short-term experiment, the chassis being classified 4/9 STL like all the others, even when new. They were converted to standard after only a year or two.

Direct injection was an important new feature of 132 more STL buses built in the summer of 1939. These were STL 2516–2647, classified 15 STL 16, and represented the ultimate development of the class, though not the end of its story. London Transport had persevered with indirect injection for longer than most British bus operators, evidently reasoning that the greater performance—the standard A171 7·7-litre engine could give 115 bhp at 2000 rpm—and slightly smoother running justified the higher fuel consumption. But the economic advantages of the direct injection A173 version of the same engine, introduced on an experimental basis in some operators fleets in 1936, finally persuaded even LT to use it in the 15 STLs.

Although the A173 engine was slightly rougher running in itself, as installed in the 15 STL chassis less noise and vibration reached the interior of the bodywork. This was because of the use of fully-flexible engine mountings, a feature of the newly-introduced RT-type, but non-standard on an 0661-type Regent. In fact the 15 STL 16 buses were pleasant to ride in. The maximum power of the A173 engine was about 95 bhp, but the difference was partly accounted for by a reduction in governed speed, so little differ-ence was evident in traffic driving. Originally the 15 STL chassis had deeper radiators and wheel discs, but these features tended to vanish on subsequent overhaul. The bodies looked the same as STL 12 and 14 but incorporated more metal parts in the framing. Some were allocated to the country area, being the first green rear-entrance STLs, but, later, a few examples of most types were repainted green.

The next step was the conversion of the petrol 56-seat STLs that had preselective gearboxes to oil, using A173 direct-injection engines on flexible mountings, as on the 15 STL type. Basically, the 50 3 STL 2 (STL 203–252) became 16 STL 18/1, all but three of STL 253–291 changed from 4 STL 3/2 to 1/16 STL 18 (36 converted) and the 200 7 STL 3/2 became 2/16 STL 18 (vehicle numbers STL 403–552 and 559–608). In practice, the bodies had been interchanged between these types on overhaul, so both STL 18 and 18/1 were to be found on examples of all batches converted. The three buses not converted from petrol to oil were STL 253, 263 and 290, which had been converted to syncromesh gearboxes (amidships gearbox mounting) experimentally in 1937—they might well have been the first synchromesh double-deckers in Britain. They do not appear to have impressed LT, being converted to crash gearbox in 1939 and thus excluded from the diesel conversion.

London Transport had ceased building spare bodies in 1938. But the earlier spares came in very useful after 1939, when war-damaged vehicles and repair facilities lacking or diverted to other uses upset the previous system. Twelve new bodies classified STL 17, outwardly similar to the standard STLs of the 1937–39 period, but having wood-framed seats and internal panelling as on the STL 3 type of 1933–34, were built late in 1941. All but three went on to existing chassis, between STL 258 and STL 2621.

By the time the last three were ready, London Transport had received some of its allocation of 34 AEC Regent chassis under the Government's "unfrozen" vehicle scheme for the completion of bus chassis for which parts

were in stock—these were of AEC's basic standard design of the time, with A173 engine mounted almost rigidly and D124 crash gearbox. These were given the numbers STL 2648–2681 and classified 17 STL.

A corresponding number of bodies were put in hand at the Chiswick works—14 more STL 17/1, similar to the dozen STL 17 mentioned above but with no roof route number box and no rear indicators, and 20 of a quite new low-height STL 19 version based on the standard STL in general appearance. But only 13 of the STL 17/1 plus the three remaining STL 17 were fitted to the new chassis. The remaining 18 of the 17 STL received existing bodies, including two 60-seat bodies dating from 1933, as well as some examples only a couple of years old. The bodies had to be modified to suit the 17 STL chassis and thus were created two STL 1/1, one STL 2/1, two STL 3/3, one STL 3/4, two STL 5/3, four STL 11/1, four STL 14/2, and

94

two STL 12/1. STL 1/1, STL 3/3 and STL 3/4 duplicated earlier codes. Surprisingly enough, this random selection was not subsequently altered—in fact body transfers virtually ceased from early in the war period until the last STLs were withdrawn. All the 17 STLs were at first painted red, but always ran in the country area, being used on hilly routes, later becoming green.

The 20 lowbridge STL 19 bodies, which seated 53 (27 up, 26 down) again on 1933–4 style seats, were fitted to standard STL chassis between STL 1617 and 2311. Twelve were red and eight green, for use on routes with restricted headroom. These were the last production bodies built at Chiswick, the last being completed in 1943, though one experimental metal-framed highbridge body was built for STL 2477 after the war.

But development work did not stop, and in 1942 a programme to convert the indirect-injection A171 engines fitted to most STLs

Left: The interior of a 1937 STL does not look unduly dated 35 years later. This view is of one of the Park Royal-built STL 15 bodied with half-round section pillars. Note the good forward vision. *Right:* Not what it seems. This is STL 2674, one of the "unfrozen" crash gearbox chassis delivered in 1942, and in this case fitted with 60-seat LGOC body dating from 1933, the resulting vehicle being coded 17 STL 1/1.

Right: One of the last production bodies to be produced by Chiswick Works was this STL 19 low-height 53-seater built in 1943 and fitted to a 1937 4/9 STL chassis, STL 2229.

to A173 direct-injection standard was put in hand. Some 2150 engines were involved and the work was not completed until at least 1947. It seems possible that some of the planned conversions were never carried out. Fuel economy was important in those days and the standard power setting was 86 bhp—well down on the original output, but performance with the fast changes of the pre-selector gearbox was better than might have thought and the STL was generally a nimble bus. The Godstone STLs were also converted to direct injection.

The last additions to the STL class were 20 more crash gearbox buses built in 1945–46 to AECs Regent Mark II design, which differed only in braking system to the "unfrozen" buses of 1941–42. These received standard Weymann metal-framed bodies, complete with such non-London features as outswept skirt panels, and were coded 18 STL 20 and numbered STL 2682–2701.

A final chapter in the STL story was the elaborate conversion of the 1939 15 STL and later some 4/9 STL chassis to accept RT-type bodywork, the resulting vehicles being numbered SRT. This is outside the scope of this article, but a consequence was conversion of other 4/9 STL chassis, mostly from the STL 2014–2188 batch originally fitted with Park Royal bodies, to take the 1939 STL 16 bodies rendered surplus by the SRT conversion. These vehicles were classified 19 STL 16/2 and about 60 had been produced by the summer of 1949.

Withdrawal of STL-class buses got under way in earnest after 1950. Lack of normal body maintenance during the war had taken its toll. Many vehicles had been extensively reconditioned, mainly by Mann Egerton, and others more crudely patched up with external strapping, but diminishing vehicle needs accelerated the end. By 1954 all had gone, but even so, many STLs lasted for 17 years or more, compared to a probable intended life of not more than 10.

In addition to various published sources, I would like to acknowledge the help of Mr. Colin Curtis and Mr. Gavin Martin in compiling this article.

95

Municipal muster/2: north-east England

Photographs by G. COXON

Above left: West Hartlepool Bristol RELL/ECW and Leyland Leopard/Strachans buses. Below left: A Teesside Daimler CRL6 with Northern Counties 70-seat bodywork.

Above: Barrow Corporation has a batch of these Leyland PD2s with Massey forward-entrance bodies. Below: A Darlington Daimler Roadliner with two-door Roe body.

Box Brownie to yesterday

Photographs by GAVIN BOOTH

Fifteen years of photographing buses might seem a comparatively short time, but a flick back through some Box Brownie photos from my schoolboy days serves as a reminder of just how many elderly buses could be seen in all parts of the country—buses that would now be eagerly prized by any preservationist.

These two veterans were still in active service with Alexanders at Falkirk in June 1962. They are an all-Leyland Titan TD5 and a Daimler CWA6 utility.

Below left: The Alexander fleet still contained many oddities in the 1960s, like a batch of these Leyland Cheetahs with Burlingham bodies—albeit with nasty full fronts. K32 at Kirkcaldy in August 1960. *Below:* This 1938 AEC Regal with original rear-entrance Alexander body had just arrived in Edinburgh on the express service from Glasgow (!) one busy Saturday in July 1960.

The last Leyland Titan TD2s operating in Britain were the ECW-bodied and 5LW-engined examples of Eastern Counties, like this one seen at Woodbastwick in July 1960.

In August 1961, in addition to Guy Arabs and Leyland TD5s, Bournemouth Corporation had vintage trolleybuses like this 1935 Sunbeam MS2/Park Royal. On the left is an ex-Brighton BUT/Weymann.

Below left: Edinburgh Corporation had a sizeable fleet of these elderly Daimler COG5s running until they were replaced by Leyland Tiger Cubs in 1959. This one, 655, dated from 1938. *Below:* A breakdown on the Glasgow tram system—but it was postwar Cunarder 1336 which had broken down, and 1902 standard car 488 had pushed it on to an unused section of track. April 1961.

Nell Gwynne, forerunners, friends and followers

J. E. DUNABIN recalls halcyon days in Herefordshire

Not very long ago enthusiasm for the motor bus and for its widespread activities was almost a secret religion, something one kept hidden from all but ones nearest and dearest —and even from them at times. Now, it has been publicly acknowledged by so many people that some quite surprising variants on the theme are gaining credibility, and one can risk confessing a passionate devotion to a collection of vehicles distinguishable only, by the uninitiated, from many others by the colour of their paint. Anguished laments have been heard for the passing of "Silver

Star", for "Brown Bombers", Ledgards of Leeds and others.

But with all the riches that remain, in Bishop Auckland, in Doncaster, and in many other places from Caithness to Cornwall, and the many exciting episodes of the past fifty years or more to savour, in London for example or in Stoke-on-Trent, served at one time or another by over two hundred—yes 200—operators, why pick on Herefordshire, where few people meant few buses? Motor omnibuses, though not all the same—here one steers a careful course between those who

regard them all as tin boxes and those for whom each PD2 has a soul—do not exhibit great regional variations, so why not concentrate on where there are and were plenty of them? And the early bus operators too, though speaking with varying accents, seem to have had more in common personally than they differed regionally. The answer may have to be like that of the mountaineers, climbing mountains "just because they are there", or possibly just because *I* was there.

Herefordshire is a beautiful part of England, a peaceful land of cider orchards, half-timbered buildings, hopyards, and the famous whitefaced cattle. Its people are proud of their county, though hardly—dare it be said?—possessing that intense devotion to its institutions and activities manifested by Londoners, Scotsmen and natives of Yorkshire. Perhaps the cult of the motor bus should be confined to the territory served by the B type, the K, the NS, and their successors,

with outposts in Airdrie, the West Riding, and possibly County Durham.

But let us take another look. The county where, a few years after passage of the Road Traffic Act of 1930, the advancing age of one horse was mentioned as a reason for extending a motor service, where one of the earliest attempts was made to run extended tours with a chain of hotels owned by the operator, and where one of the most famous of bus designers remained as director of a bus company long after he had apparently severed all connections with the operating side of the industry, has perhaps got something special. And it was here, when one of the greatest bus companies gave up motors in favour of horses, that one of its redundant vehicles was taken into service by a pioneer independent. The ultimate destiny of many a motor bus has lain in a field, serving as a home for hens. In Herefordshire, so a local story goes, the process was reversed, when a henhouse

Left: The yard of "The Black Lion", Hereford, half a century ago. All three vehicles are Brush-bodied Tilling Stevens TS3s.

This lorry bus, a Model T Ford, belonged to Mr W. G. Morris. It is pictured loading for Longtown in Hereford.

101

was taken out of a field and mounted on a platform lorry to convert the latter into a passenger carrier.

These were of course events of long ago. If we turn to more recent times, different but equally striking facts can be noted. In the early postwar period, north-west Herefordshire and the areas beyond its boundaries enjoyed, until harsh economic pressures destroyed it, a network of regular daily bus services such as no other area so devoid of people can have experienced. A new market service was started too, coming admittedly from over the border in Breconshire, which took three hours to reach Hereford.

Much later—to write "even now" would be tempting fate—a very different approach by another operator has kept bus services running in the south-western sector of the county in defiance of the general trend. And lest anybody should think of these Herefordians as stuck in their red clinging soil, with rare excursions to Barry or Blackpool, mention should be made of a real long distance operator, a post-World War II pioneer, who grew up almost literally in the shadow of another notable, one of the liveliest independents in the whole of the Welsh Border and West Midlands too, and then reached out from Credenhill to Khatmandu.

Forty years ago, however, when I first surveyed the Herefordshire scene, these things were still to come, and there were no signs of what had gone before. Connellys, who purchased 0 1278, a Milnes-Daimler double-decker, by auction at the BMMO garage, Five Ways, Birmingham, in September 1908, gave up the struggle after their current vehicle caught fire—smoking and filling up with petrol, then as now, were incompatible activities—in 1912, leaving Hereford "bus-less" for some years. Mr. Caws' finely conceived tours business, with two charabancs, a Ford and a Garford, hotels in the Isle of Wight, Llandrindod Wells, Dinas Dinlle in Caernarvonshire, and at his Ross on Wye headquarters, had collapsed, to be reborn in reduced form elsewhere. Frank Searle disappeared from the board of Hereford Transport Ltd., still known as Howell's Yellow

Buses, in about 1924, leaving no obvious imprint on bus services in Herefordshire. Nevertheless the magic was still there, or so it seemed, sustained by the pioneers from the early lorry bus days, and enhanced by the doings of others who had joined in later.

Although Herefordshire has always been rather thin from a traffic point of view, it still attracted the big battalions. BMMO established themselves in the city as early as 1920, Bristol Tramways came into the county soon afterwards, and Crosville appeared in the north-western corner of Herefordshire in 1924. Midland Red men, at most levels, stayed somewhat aloof from the locals, whose ways in many cases would not have met with Mr. O. C. Power's approval, and whose buses were, euphemistically, a mixed lot. Crosville, however, soon after the 1930 Act became operative, reached an agreement with Yeomans Motors of Canon Pyon to avoid conflict between Kington and New Radnor, and provide better connections between Hereford and Llandrindod Wells. Even earlier than this, in mid 1929, the Bristol company established a joint service between Hereford and Gloucester with Hereford Transport Ltd. This latter company, originally locally based and with a flavour all its own, owing much to Mr. E. W. Howell's desire to lessen the isolation of rural communities, was then being metamorphosed, with others controlled by Mr. J. H. Watts and his associates, from "independent" to "area" company.

Relationships between Hereford Transport and the smaller independents were good, and remained so after the take-over. Mrs. Capper, who with great energy ran a bus business and other related activities from one of the recognised "principal seats" in the county, using its name, "The Northgate", to identify her buses, called on Mr. Watts of Lydney when she was short of a vehicle. Her successor, Mr. G. Jorden, took services over from Hereford Transport and ran them for eight or nine years before returning them, with all his others, to Red & White.

Another operator in the same area, Mr. F. T. Hammond of Kingsthorne, one of whose services competed with those of Red

& White, acquired second-hand buses from that company, and drivers too, though on a different basis it is assumed. For other non-competing routes a specially narrow body was supplied by Watts of Lydney.

One could not expect amity to persist where the driver for one bus owner left and set up on his own, competing directly with his former employer, and the existence elsewhere of two market services from the same village to Hereford, though by different routes, meant that relations between the two providers were a little strained. This was only a faint echo of the situation in many other parts of the country, where cut-throat competition was the rule; here in Herefordshire conflicts were few, and in general friendliness prevailed, to mutual advantage.

With small fleets and no spare vehicles breakdowns or major overhauls created a need for borrowing. Market days had been fixed long before the advent of the motor bus, but careful avoidance of competition between neighbouring towns was a boon to the busman when he did arrive. One bus could go to Abergavenny on Tuesday, Hereford on Wednesday, Hay on Thursday, Abergavenny again on Friday, and finish off the week with a market journey and an evening cinema trip to Hereford on Saturday. This was on the western side of the county; in the east the Tuesday, Thursday and Friday placenames were different but the pattern was the same.

If the bus was not available on Wednesday then the net had to be cast wide to find somebody with no commitments for that day. Mr. Pritchard of Michaelchurch looked west over the country boundary to Mr. Blackwell of Llanvihangel Crucorney, whose big day was Tuesday, and the blue/white Dodge of Honddu Valley Motor Services could occasionally be seen on Pritchard's Longtown to Hereford route. Various other standing arrangements existed, most of them two-way but not all. Occasionally A's buses were good enough for B but not vice versa.

Weddings had to take place on the bridegroom's free day of course, and on such occasions a bus was a very handy thing to have, provided somebody else competent to drive could be found. Within the county at least, distance appears to have been no object. A picture exists of a Herefordshire bus, tastefully decorated for the owner's wedding, he himself in front, with another operator and three spare drivers ranged alongside.

With a bus on loan usually went a driver, transferring his loyalty temporarily, or was it just unity in the face of a common enemy? One retired driver, having many subsequent years of loyal service with the "opposition" to his credit, recalls being questioned closely as to his destination by Midland Red men ready to chase his elderly bus, and then use the technique, not unknown outside Herefordshire, of darting ahead to cream off the traffic. The answer, "To Symonds Yat" (a well known destination for pleasure trips), enabled him to proceed to his true destination undisturbed, and to do much better for the hirer of his employer's vehicle.

Mention has been made of a postwar service to Khatmandu. This was probably the furthest point reached by a Herefordshire bus, but there had been other forays well outside the county much earlier. A service to

A Bedford WLB, Duple bodied, new to Mr W. Pritchard of Longtown in 1932, pictured here in the livery of Mr E. E. Williams.

London started in 1919 was withdrawn as soon as the railway strike which had led to its introduction ended, but a regular summer week-end service by charabanc to Aberystwyth lasted, in spite of many difficulties. One of these, the absence of filling stations en route, was overcome by carrying 24 two-gallon tins of petrol to Builth Wells on the forward journey.

The tremendous activity in opening up long distance services which gathered force in the late 1920s also had its echoes in Herefordshire. Mr. W. E. Morgan's buses, which already ran between Hereford and Leominster, appeared in Shrewsbury in May 1930, competing with a Midland Red service from Hereford which started on the same day. Shortly afterwards Mr. P. B. Davies of Bodenham, already running local services, went even further afield with a regular service between Cardiff and Blackpool via Hereford. Mr. Morgan chose "Wye

Valley Motors" as a fleetname. Mr. Davies identified his vehicles with one of Hereford's best-known daughters. It was inevitable when a question was raised concerning the whereabouts of some member of the opposite sex, and answered by "He's gone to Blackpool with Nell Gwynne", that some misunderstanding should arise. Nell Gwynne visited Blackpool frequently during the next few summers.

There were many local competitors in the race which started in 1920, and the handicap for late entry during the next few years was slight. Two basic rules governed the contest. One said that you should not compete with an earlier established independent over all or even a large part of his route. This rule was occasionally broken, but observance did make it easier to conform with the other one, which said that you should pick up enough passengers to make the service pay, even if it meant pursuing a very devious route to town.

A wartime picture of an M type SOS in Hereford.

Right: Another wartime view, this time of Yeomans VJ 7405, one of three AEC Regals acquired in 1935.

Persisting with the analogy, the field had thinned a little by 1931, when the Road Traffic Act of 1930 began to take effect, and was quite spread out. The leaders were Wye Valley and Yeomans Motors, neither with very big fleets (less than ten in each case) but each acting as if they had big futures. Behind them came some smaller businesses, energetically run, with the really "small men", owner drivers, tough and energetic but not so ambitious, bringing up the rear.

One of this last group was obviously not prepared to go along with the new system. His original "Application to continue" stage operation only specified terminal points, and no route. A sad note in a later set of *Notices and Proceedings* stated that no licence had been granted owing to the failure of the applicant to provide the required information. This was an isolated case, and although one or two Herefordshire bus operators needed reminders about the requirements of the 1930

Act in respect of their vehicles, very few real difficulties arose.

In retrospect this is a little surprising. Farming communities rarely like being governed, and Herefordshire busmen who stayed close to home had no previous experience of any form of service licensing. Perhaps it was self confidence, a Herefordshire attribute with which they all seemed endowed in good measure, which made them feel they could take such things in their stride.

The Act did produce a few minor upheavals in the county, and one major battle. This concerned two of the most recently established but potentially very rewarding services, those running between Hereford and Shrewsbury. Attempts by the Birmingham company to steam-roller were unsuccessful, only resulting in neither operator getting what he wanted. Wisdom then prevailed, and unopposed applications by each, with co-ordinated timings, followed.

Slowly the Herefordshire bus scene, which was colourful but a bit patchy, took on a more modern appearance. Leaders in the field were again the two biggest independents. Red & White, however, achieved two local "firsts" which, though far less spectacular than "Yeomans Radio Coach", both represented solid achievement. One was a heated bus, which made its winter users the envy of many travellers. And this was not an "off the shelf" fitment—it is doubtful whether there were many *on* the shelf at the time—but a locally-installed system. The other was the operation of the first diesel-engined bus from Hereford. This vehicle created some amusement locally because of its reluctance to start. It could not leave the depot on its own, but had to wait for another bus to come in to provide a tow. Up the street, once round the war memorial and back to the depot was usually enough.

Dieselisation did not stop there of course.

More buses with the new and noisy engines appeared, and the increased power they developed encouraged a certain amount of time-saving. A favourite run, after a little time-killing, was from the top of the Callow Pitch down to Hereford seven miles away, and here drivers had the effrontery to overtake Black & White "express" vehicles on the Cheltenham to Hereford service.

Racing did occur elsewhere too, Herefordshire, like other places, having its recognised courses. Things had begun to warm up in the middle 1920s as new and faster vehicles became available. The Fiats and Fords could easily outstrip the Daimlers and Tilling-Stevens on the flat, but as buses became faster and police attention closer, flat racing had to be forgotten and competitors took to the hills. There were the Callow, where one could race up as well as down, Dinmore Hill, and others. Even the wisdom of the Traffic Commissioners could do little about spacing out

school buses, and as a rather slow SOS lumbered up the Seven Stars Pitch from Madley, it was not too difficult for a Red & White Albion to slip past.

Herefordshire people, with memories of what had gone before—very little other than horse-drawn carriers carts—were well pleased with their buses, which gave them as frequent service as their few numbers could support, and rarely let them down. Outsiders, used to better things, or at least more frequent buses, but without understanding, were more critical. World War II gave Herefordshire operators the chance to demonstrate what they could do when the demand was really there.

Hereford's bus station, which from its opening a few years earlier had never looked busy except on market days, began to take on a different appearance. Queues formed, largely of men in grey blue uniform, and strange—strange that is to Herefordshire ears —accents were heard. Strange buses appeared

too, an odd-looking TSM destined for Hong Kong originally but now in the Wye Valley livery of crimson/maroon, a Gilford, possibly the first resident of this make, and, oddest of all, a Bedford with a full-fronted lorry cab and a body taken from an older bus.

The queues grew longer, and prodigious efforts were made to clear them. The bus station, if not exactly a popular place, certainly became more populous, even up to the late hours of Saturday and Sunday nights.

Peace came, and the queues shrank, but Herefordshire was never going to be the same again. Nor, apparently, were its buses. The uniforms remained prominent in city and bus station; so did the strange accents. Camps built for military personnel were used to house other people, refugees from far away places. With no roots in Herefordshire soil, they looked to the city for many things and travelled there, by bus of course. Wye Valley buses brought them in from the west, while

Left: An ex-Glasgow Corporation Cowieson-bodied Leyland TD1 operated by Yeomans from 1940 onwards.

A Bedford VAM service bus of Yeomans about to depart from Credenhill (old railway station).

Messrs. Yeomans provided a similar service from points on or near their main route between Kington and Hereford. Up in the north of the county Primrose Motor Services, who had helped to make Hereford busier during wartime, now focussed their attention on Leominster, starting several new services. Herefordshire on the whole was becoming more mobile, attracted by the magnet of an expanding county town and to a lesser extent the smaller towns.

One should not belittle the part played by the major transport companies, although it must be mentioned that Crosville buses have vanished from the county, Western Welsh have come and gone, and Red & White Services Ltd., although succeeding to a number of former "Bristol" operations, are rather less prominent relatively than their predecessors must have been over 40 years ago. Midland Red buses have served Herefordshire for over 50 years, and they continue to

brighten the city streets. Most of those seen, however, are not destined for anywhere further away than the suburbs.

The difficulties of rural bus operators in making ends meet mounted with the rise in car ownership from the middle 1950s on, and well-informed observers were doubting as long as a decade ago, whether they could survive for long without immediate and substantial reliefs or subsidies. As we move further into the 1970s, few surely would begrudge praise to G. H. Yeomans Motors of Canon Pyon for one of the best stage carriage fleets anywhere, nor to Wye Valley Motors for maintaining so well their rural service network in an area with plenty of scenery but few people. Whatever may happen after these thoughts have been committed to paper, one can still speculate whether conditions that have been right for growing apples, hops, and other fruits of the earth, may be right for running buses too.

A new Leyland Leopard, en route from Cheltenham, seen in Hereford in October 1971.

The decline and fall of the trolleybus

Photographs by G. COXON and R. L. WILSON

The days of the trolleybus have been numbered for some time, but there were still fifteen British trolleybus operators in 1967 and it seems surprising that only five years later there should be none at all.

As recently as 1961/1962 Reading and Bournemouth Corporations were buying modern, efficient trolleybuses —the last two Bournemouth trolleybuses only entered service in November 1962—but their lifespan was to be short.

Now trolleybuses have joined street tramways as mere memories in Britain. The trolleybus has had a relatively short and undistinguished career in this country; it gave good service, but was largely overtaken by other events and pressures.

Luckily there is a small army of preserved trolleybuses, and there are plans to establish a working museum which should ensure that the trolleybus is not forgotten.

Some of the newest trolleybuses to enter service in Britain were Sunbeam/Weymann vehicles like Bournemouth 265 seen here.

A Karrier W of 1947 with Roe 56-seat bodywork, in service with South Shields Corporation.

One of the smart Burlingham-bodied Sunbeam F4As acquired by Teesside from Reading Corporation.

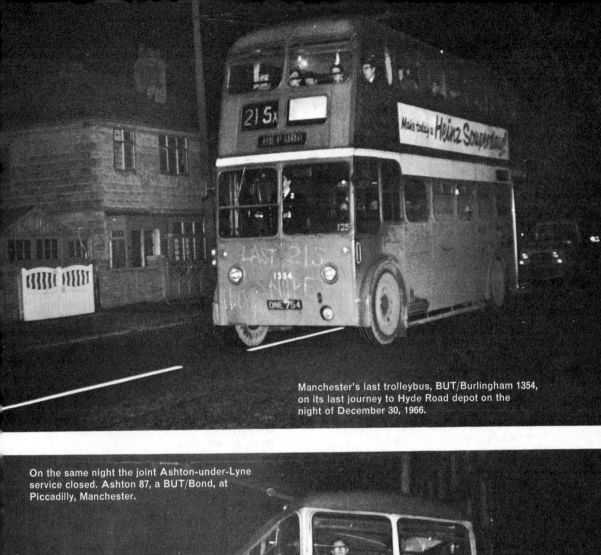

Manchester's last trolleybus, BUT/Burlingham 1354, on its last journey to Hyde Road depot on the night of December 30, 1966.

On the same night the joint Ashton-under-Lyne service closed. Ashton 87, a BUT/Bond, at Piccadilly, Manchester.

One of Glasgow's 1958 Crossley-bodied BUT
9613Ts in its original livery, in 1966.

One of Hull's unusual Roe-bodied Sunbeams, on
service in 1961.

Glimpses of richness in the Potteries

A. MOYES on the recent bus scene in North Staffordshire

One of a pair of Burlingham-bodied AEC Reliances which passed into the PMT fleet from Baxter, Hanley, heaves itself up the 1 in 7 of Penkhull New Road, with Stoke as a backcloth.

In the magazine *Buses* for March 1967, some thoughts were offered on the attractiveness of North Staffordshire for the bus enthusiast. At the time, there was a fairly obvious wealth of interesting vehicles at large in the Stoke-on-Trent conurbation, in the liveries of the dominant Potteries Motor Traction (PMT) and the six independent stage-carriage operators which survived in the conurbation. It was recognised that this richness was relative to a national picture of increasing standardisation of vehicles. Superficially comparing 1972 with, say, 1962, North Staffordshire's psv endowment might now seem positively bland and flavourless. Yet currently there remain odd glimpses of the richness of yesterday. The last three years in particular represented a most stimulating period, enriched at times with a host of varied PMT hirelings dotting the often characterful streets of the Potteries and its rural surroundings. This article seeks to convey something of the flavour of the 1967–1972 period in the area, and what of psv interest may still be seen there.

PMTs plans for standardisation in the late

1960s seemed likely to sweep the fleet clear of the remnants of the fleets of numerous independents which it had absorbed in the postwar period, as well as individual batches of non-standard vehicles it had itself bought in the 1950s. 1967 had seen the end of PMTs attractive AEC Regents with Northern Counties bodywork and the dozen Guy Arab/Orion deckers. It had also witnessed the withdrawal of such idiosyncrasies as H495, a Leyland *Tiger* double-decker (of which more anon), a Carmarthenshire-registered Guy Arab single-decker, and one of the few Dennis Lancet UF coaches built. Forty-two new Daimler Roadliner saloons, bodied by Plaxton and Marshall, provided a somewhat tame replacement, apart from the Lotus-like sound effects from their Cummins engines. The next year was little better, as the pair of Bedford SB8s which had been incorporated from the

113

fleet of Stanier, Newchapel, in 1965 also were withdrawn. Despite their coach bodies (one Yeates, one Duple), these had done quite a bit of stage-carriage work in their three years with PMT. Indeed, SL997 had even had a tall bus indicator perched atop its Duple coachwork. With a diminishing number of independents left in the area to absorb, and attrition of its own batches of older vehicles, the PMT fleet seemed inevitably doomed to standardisation. Further Roadliners, and single-deck Fleetlines, were either on order or in the course of delivery. It was partly because of delays in the delivery of these that the most unexpected incident in the recent psv history of the conurbation occurred—the hiring of vehicles from a variety of operators.

The first vehicles to be hired by PMT were probably the most noteworthy visitors to North Staffordshire, and indeed as a type they virtually outlasted the other hired specimens. In an area which had lost its last PMT half-cab single-deckers some six years previously, it was astonishing suddenly to see vehicles of this type apparently everywhere in the conurbation one day in June 1969. In fact there were rarely more than half-a-dozen of them in the Potteries at any one time, all being Birmingham Corporation Leyland PS2/1s with distinctive B34F bodies by Metro-Cammell. Whatever one's views might be on recessed windscreens, one could not but be impressed by their gleaming blackberry blue livery, their chromed radiators, and their turn of speed (the latter thanks to a high power-to-weight ratio). Throughout the following twelve months they would turn up unexpectedly in scattered parts of the company's territory—such as at Eccleshall on route 51 from Newcastle, or at Alsager in Cheshire on the 20. At the New Year some of them returned south to reappear with West Midlands pte stickers over their Birmingham crests. I vividly remember witnessing a run by 2247 on the Tunstall-Newcastle circular route no. 27 almost at the end of its sojourn in the area, on a rainy Saturday in May 1970. From Tunstall this run forsakes the main roads of the conurbation and dives off into no-man's land; 2247 splashed through

the deluge in a brisk descent into the Fowlea valley, levelling out to pass the flaming cupola of the now-closed Goldendale Ironworks on its left. At this somewhat desolate spot the other vehicle working the service, in the clockwise direction, was crossed—a Trent Tiger Cub. 2247 then could be heard splashing away through the rain, and then making short work of the fierce climb up the western side of the valley, its fairly rounded rump retreating into the downpour.

The half-dozen Trent Tiger Cubs seemed rather prosaic in comparison, although their dual-purpose bodywork offered perhaps a little more comfort for the average passenger. Their exterior appearance was a curious compromise of curvaceous red side panels and precious styling details on the basic BET Federation stage-carriage shape of the early 1960s. They had superseded a further half-dozen Tiger Cubs from East Midland in that dull red of theirs which made the Metro-Cammell-bodied versions among the most drab in the conurbation. The Willowbrook-bodied contingent was, on the other hand, a rather more attractive shape and the frontal appearance was broken by the simple winged motif then favoured by that builder. It was unusual to see and photograph R39 leaving Keele University on the PMT contract to Newcastle in July 1969 as it was not one of their normal rosters; in fact these vehicles seemed to stray from the main routes rather less than the PS2s. Making up numbers when the latter were temporarily returned to Birmingham were handfuls of AEC Reliance coaches from Sheffield United Tours, which again were rarely away from the inner areas of the PMT territory. By June 1971, delivery of some long-awaited Alexander-bodied Fleetline single-deckers had nearly been completed, and the faithful PS2s returned south for the last time. With the dispatch of Western Welsh Reliance coaches 133/7–9 back home at the end of October 1970, the hirings as a whole were concluded.

Talking of Leyland PS2s, an occasional glimpse of a Tiger in an inappropriate guise could be obtained until mid-1967. PMTs love of the idiosyncratic was well expressed

114

In a downpour, West Midlands pte Leyland PS2 2247, on hire to PMT, passes the Goldendale Ironworks on the Talke Pits circular in May 1970.

A typical PMT "mongrel" of the 1950s. The full story of H495 is in this article.

After a low bridge accident, PMT fitted a home-made roof to this ex-Baxter Leyland Titan/Willowbrook, seen in Newcastle.

in H495 which, as the photograph shows, was superficially an ordinary Titan but in fact had a curious lineage. Its chassis was a PS2/3 which had passed into the fleet in 1954 with the business of H. Davies of Stoke. As with many of the area's independents, Davies was loyal to the several local small-scale bodybuilders, and OEH 700 originally boasted a typical half-cab body by Hassall. It was not long before this was replaced by a rather heavy-looking Northern Counties double-deck affair lifted from a rebodied prewar PMT Titan. The resultant H495 was rather camera-shy, but I managed a ride on it once off the home ground of its native Burslem depot, on the Hanley-Newcastle trunk route. Despite not having been designed for its eventual burden, it performed so easily on the difficult Basford Bank that tape-recordings of its sound effects were unrewarding. All that was captured was an odd gearbox surge and a good deal of body creaking. At that time, there was a further pair of "Tigers" of an indirect sort remaining in the fleet—indirect in that they were in reality export OPD2/1 Titan chassis which were new in 1949 with 8ft wide Weymann single-deck bodies. Along with eight other brethren, SN 466 and 467 received new Northern Counties double-decker bodywork in 1954, of a squarer outline than that on H495, but

still quite attractive. As L466, one of the pair survives as the PMT driver training vehicle, albeit rebuilt without stairs, and at the time of writing can still be found parked by the Stoke depot when not in use.

At the time of writing the PMT fleet still contains operational examples from fleets acquired in the 1960s. Most local independents have generally maintained quite up-to-date studs of first-hand vehicles, as Turner, Poole and Proctor currently illustrate. Thus PMT have often been recipients of vehicles with reasonable life-expectancy. Some of the most persistent second-hand acquisitions came from Baxter's, of Hanley, at the end of 1958. Early in 1970, a pair of their Burlingham-bodied Reliances was still busily circulating around the City of Stoke-on-Trent. S677 appeared fairly often on the exacting route 5, which served by-roads between Hanley and Stoke, then to heave itself up the precipitous Penkhull New Road en route for the suburbs of Springfields, (see photograph). Its brother S678 received a modified front end as shown in *Buses Illustrated* no. 144, but both were withdrawn in October 1970.

116

PMT H6650, an MCW-bodied Daimler CVG6, threads past gasworks and level crossings on a temporary diversion.

A pair of Baxter's Willowbrook-bodied Titans, dating from 1955 and 1957 respectively, boasted long life in PMT ownership. L510 also succumbed in late 1970, having in the interim received a top deck of PMT design and manufacture to replace its original, which had been swept off in a difference of opinion with Glebe Street railway bridge. L679 surprisingly managed to hang on well into the area of farebox one-man double-deckers and could still be seen late in 1971 plying the Longton-Newcastle route at peak hours. With its withdrawal, the last of the really distinctive second-hand buses in the PMT fleet will have disappeared. A front-entranced Leyland PD3, ordered by Baxter but delivered after the PMT takeover, survives, as do a Northern Counties-bodied Fleetline H992 (83XEH), ex-Beckett, Bucknall, which is superficially identical to a contemporary batch of PMT Fleetlines, and a most curious Tiger Cub/Seagull coach, converted to one-man operation, formerly with Stanier, Newchapel. In addition, one of the three Reliances with Willowbrook bodies, intended for City of Oxford but placed into service with Wells Motor Services Ltd., a PMT subsidiary wound up in 1959, remains in service at Biddulph depot. Solace must therefore be sought among the fleets of the six independent stage-carriage operators of the conurbation.

Such a search could probably be made best in a journey one could start at the northern end of the City of Stoke-on-Trent. Here, at Goldenhill, was the northern limit of the Potteries Electric Traction tram system, with a small car shed, now demolished, marking the highest point on the network at 731ft O.D. Interest today would focus on the depot of Stoniers which remains at Goldenhill though their main sphere of operation is now further south in the City. Stonier has for long favoured second-hand double-deckers for his stage work, which involves a share in a high-frequency suburban route from Hanley. Leyland Titan PD2s were favoured until mid-1971 when two AEC Regent Vs (one from Hebble, one from Yorkshire Woollen) arrived. Shortly after, 961 GBF, a PD3/4/Massey was bought from neighbouring independent,

Turner of Brown Edge. To add to variety, a pair of ex-City of Oxford Dennis Lolines (301/2 KFC) was being prepared for service in November 1971.

Although the conurbation is heavily industrialised, there are very few special buses provided for works or colliery use by firms themselves or by independents. Possibly this can be ascribed to the close juxtaposition of housing and industry, so that journeys-to-work are relatively short; many of these flows are readily catered for by the close-headway services which thread the conurbation. However, Stoniers do provide a miners service across the edge of the city to the Chatterley Whitfield colliery, on which ex-Hills, Tredegar saloon 115 GAX is often used. Just south of Goldenhill, at the Old Boston Pottery alongside the A50 trunk road are stabled two double-deckers run by Staffordshire Potteries Ltd. Their relatively new factory at Meir on the south-eastern edge of the city attracts some labour from the northern side; ex-Leicester Leyland PD2 FJF 160 and AEC Regent/Massey FAV 826 (ex-Alexanders Northern, but originally part of the Sutherland, Peterhead fleet) provide subsidised transport. They are one of the few manufacturers in the conurbation to do so.

Moving south, Tunstall, the northernmost of the Five Towns, is dominated by PMT, as is the next town, Burslem, less than two miles away. Between them, and providing vehicles for both, is PMTs Burslem depot, which features some of the company's recent dual-entrance Bristol RELL6Ls with ECW coachwork. Modernisation does not evidently mean standardisation! It would be appropriate from Burslem to take the hourly service 130 south-westwards to Silverdale to view the next contingent of independents. One would descend to Longport, passing ,a fine bottle kiln at Price's teapot works by the Trent & Mersey canal en route, and then (if one were travelling in a Roadliner) crawl up Porthill Bank before reaching easier grades. While crossing the western suburbs, now administratively in the borough of Newcastle-under-Lyme, the vehicle passes two large electrical engineering works at Milehouse

Beneath the emblem of Hanley's largest store, Stoniers PD2 LVA 483, ex-Hutchison of Overtown, splashes through a shower in 1968.

which produce considerable numbers of peak-hour extras. As well as PMT, a day-shift time attraction would be the ex-Edinburgh Leyland PD2/Orion LFS 462, owned by Sergent, of Wrinehill, a village at the western edge of the county. A solitary Crosville vehicle appears at the AEI works at the end of the day shift, on an extension of that operator's long Newcastle-Chester trunk route.

On arrival at the colliery village of Silverdale, one would have a choice of two independents' services into Newcastle proper. Princess Bus Service's Albion Aberdonian (SFW 80) and AEC Reliance 545 GVD interwork with PMT on the direct, ex-tram route, whilst Poole's Coaches of Alsagers Bank deviate via Knutton. Likely contenders for their timing would be KRF 978B or XRE 912H, Willowbrook-bodied Leopards, the former of strongly BET Federation appearance, although older Reliance/Burlingham saloons would be equally possible.

From Newcastle it is a short journey north-eastwards back into the City and the most

important of its five constituent towns— Hanley. Alternate buses on the frequent service travel indirectly via Garner Street (the original tram route, more easily graded) rather than directly, steeply and less interestingly via Basford. The former buses take the Stoke road out of Newcastle then descend gradually almost to the massive bulk of the city's gas works. Turning left along Garner Street, glimpses can be obtained into Twyford's sanitary ware works, the top deck of a Fleetline or Atlantean providing an excellent vantage point. Then one emerges onto the main Newcastle-Hanley road at Etruria station, which is followed till the rather discreet terminus at Hanley (Gitana Street). For a period in 1971, Garner Street was closed because of road works and the parallel Etruscan Street was used. This literally bisects the gas works, and some unusual photographic backgrounds for the PMT vehicles were thus on offer.

A half-mile walk across Hanley to the east side of the central area reveals the busy bus

Typical of the current fleet of Turner, Brown Edge,
is Northern Counties-bodied Daimler Fleetline 6,
seen at Hanley in May 1971.

station, which now deals with all services terminating in the town except the Newcastle group. Here in varying degrees appear the remaining independents. Stoniers, already met at Goldenhill, exhibit their second-hand stud with fair frequency. Turner of Brown Edge, now with four Northern Counties-bodied Fleetlines in an attractive dark brown/cream livery have a prosperous regular interval service to their home village. The other two independents share the Leek via Cheddleton service with PMT but the timings for which each operator is responsible are thoughtfully specified in PMTs excellent timetable booklet. Proctor of Hanley has gone 100% Fleetline also, mirroring PMTs bodywork choice of Northern Counties and Alexander. In contrast, Berresford of Cheddleton currently boasts a bevy of ex-Stockport Corporation Leyland PD2s which replaced an equally numerous purchase of ex-Salford Daimler double-deckers. Berresfords operate more stage services in the Longton area in the south-east of the City, on which ex-Silver

Star Tiger Cubs with dorsal fins appear, as does an ex-Southdown Tiger Cub which is extending one-man operation on their Longton-Leek service.

This has attempted to be no more than a superficial glimpse of psv activity in North Staffordshire. One would like to tell at length of the contractors vehicles at large in the conurbation, such as Seddon's fleet of Bristol Ls, ex-Eastern National, stabled at their Duke Street base in Fenton. PMT operations in the south-east of the City (including farebox double-deck operation at Longton) and in the unremunerative but attractive rural peripheries have been ignored. Such coach operators as Bassett of Tittensor, and Hollinshead of Scholar Green which retain some interesting vehicles, cannot receive full justice here. But the enthusiast who masters the complexities of the Potteries' urban geography will, even in these standardised days, derive a great deal of satisfaction from its still varied bus scene.

Museum pieces/2:
Edinburgh Transport Museum

GAVIN BOOTH on a praiseworthy municipal venture

Like most cities with a cultural and historical background, Edinburgh has many museums. One of the most recent—possibly the least known to the majority of citizens, far less visitors—is the Transport Museum at the front of Shrubhill Bus Works.

The withdrawal of Edinburgh Corporation's last tramcars in 1956 really started the collection off, when postwar standard car 35 was retained by the transport department when its brothers were sold for scrap, and was stored in Shrubhill pending the construction of suitable premises. Another museum piece made its first appearance at the time of the last tram operations; this was an Edinburgh & District horse bus, discovered as a chicken-coop, and beautifully restored by the transport department. This was used for publicity purposes and accompanied the last tram procession.

Here was the basis for a good collection, and it was further increased when Aberdeen Corporation offered its preserved horse tram no. 1. Ground was found in East London Street, fairly close to the Corporation's Central Garage, and a museum was built up around the exhibits. The first visitors to the new museum were members of the Omnibus Society, which held its Presidential Weekend in Scotland in 1961. These premises were only to be temporary, and following the reconstruction of Shrubhill as a modern bus works, a new purpose-built museum was constructed around tram 35, at the front of the works, just off Leith Walk. Here it remains to this day.

Tram 35 is the focal point, standing on a short length of track, complete with double-tongued point. Aberdeen horse tram 1 stands nearby, along with the horse bus. A Corporation steam roller adds variety, and recently two buses have joined the collection.

Around the walls are excellent photo-

Edinburgh tram 35 with track and point work.

panels, filled with photographs of horse, cable and electric trams, track work, buses and coaches. Other showcases contain tokens, tickets and ticket machines, uniform caps and badges, waybills, fare tables, timetables and posters. Around the wall there are the alphabetical bird and animal posters that were so familiar on Edinburgh's trams. There are tramcar drawings, crests, maps and tram and bus stops. There are models, too, showing a typical Edinburgh cable car, a Leith electric car and a demonstration model illustrating the principle of cable traction.

But the main full-size exhibits are the most attractive and the most valuable. Aberdeen horse tram 1, on Brill 21E truck, dates from the late nineteenth century, and is typical of so many cars of this era. The horse bus is finished in the blue of the time, and is still occasionally brought out for special processions or for period filming.

Electric car 35, built in 1948, is one of 84 "domed-roof standards" built at Shrubhill between 1934–1950. These attractive tramcars were 62-seaters, on Peckham P22 trucks.

The two buses in the museum are recent arrivals. In 1971 the transport department acquired RATP 3996, one of the famous Paris Renault TN4Hs, with open rear platform. 3996, a 1933 41-seater, has been repainted in a shade close to the RATP green, and carries route boards for service 68.

The other bus is very typical of Edinburgh's bus operations through the 1950s and 1960s. It is 135 (FSC 182), a 1949 Daimler CVG6 with Metro-Cammell H31/25R body, one of 72 similar buses bought in 1949/50. All but ten of this batch were fitted with Gardner 6LW engines—the remainder had Daimler CD6 engines. The Metro-Cammell bodies were built to Birmingham design to speed production—Newcastle Corporation had similar vehicles—and feature a rather dated style, complete with straight staircase. This combination of Daimler/Metro-Cammell really dated back to 1935, when the first of 51 COG6s entered service in Edinburgh, but the CVG6s were to be the last examples of this combination.

The CVG6s were the mainstay of the city bus fleet for several years, while the tram replacement Leylands and Guys arrived, but even then they continued on full-time service until large-scale with-

The Edinburgh & District Tramways Company horse bus—once a chicken coop before being restored for exhibition.

drawals started in 1964. 135 was one of the last to be withdrawn, in 1967, and is a valuable reminder of a fast disappearing type of bus.

Edinburgh's transport museum is a very worthwhile effort in a city with understandable civic pride. The fact that it concentrates on the history of one system allows greater specialisation than is normally possible—and this is something that future historians will find invaluable.

Above: The preserved Edinburgh Daimler CVG6, 135, on an enthusiasts tour, at Silverknowes on the Firth of Forth.

Top: Aberdeen horse tram 1.

Colourful years in London, 1905-1916

CHARLES F. KLAPPER, FCIT, FRGS describes early competition in London

Charles Klapper, editor of Modern Transport *from 1953 to 1968, was born in 1905 and, blessed with a father who took him about the Metropolis on business trips, was a keen observer of the London street scene from a very early age. Here he gives some idea of the colour schemes of the first years of motor bus competition, 1905 to 1916; about the same number of buses, but fewer proprietors, was involved as in the second period of intense competition between 1922 and 1934.*

The year in which I was born was distinguished by the first real impact made on the traffic of London by the motor bus. Regular services by Hancock's steam buses belonged to the 1830's; the 1890's had seen some gallant but unsuccessful experiments by

Radcliffe-Ward with battery-electric buses and the first short-lived Daimler petrol vehicles. Experimental operation continued into the beginning of this century and then an established horse bus proprietor, Thos. Tilling Ltd, decided to motorise a horse bus service and began systematic substitution of motor buses for horse buses on its famous *Times* service from Peckham to Oxford Circus, from September 29, 1904, and chose Milnes-Daimler chassis. These came basically from a German originator of the petrol-engined vehicle, but were erected in the works of an English tramcar builder, under licence. Curiously, the bodywork for Thos. Tilling was provided by another old-established horse bus operator, Birch Bros Ltd.

From at least as early as 1832 London

Left: Two green Milnes-Daimlers in the Tilling fleet on the way to the Oxford Street terminus ("Green Man and Still") of The Times route from Peckham, the first London bus route to be motorised.

A double-deck Scott-Stirling operating for London Power Ómnibus Co. Ltd. (Pioneer) on Cricklewood-Marble Arch service in 1906.

operators of horse buses had protected themselves from competition by means of associations which ran specific routes, saw that rivals had a thin time and, to be fair, saw that if receipts began to rise, more vehicles were put on the service to cope with the traffic and offer good service. They began to evolve formulae for changing over to motor buses and a little was done in this direction (the British Electric Traction group tried to buy "times" for a motor bus subsidiary in 1906) but the general opinion was that the motor bus had cut through the system and wrecked it. This was really due to the energy of the London Motor Omnibus Co Ltd, which issued a prospectus in the beginning of 1905, ordered a sizeable fleet of Milnes-Daimlers and began operations with five buses just

before I was born. They worked without respect to the carefully planned timetables of the associations at perhaps half the fare and a much greater speed—unless they broke down. They abandoned the conglomeration of painted destination names on the sides for a fleet name, Vanguard; this was intended to be a line name at first and one batch of LMO buses was named Victory; others belonged to subsidiaries with fleet names such as Arrow. A combination of popular acclaim for the Vanguard trademark and the necessity of registering a new company eventually brought all this group of vehicles under the auspices of the Vanguard Motor Omnibus Co Ltd, with the largest motor fleet in London, numbering 386.

Under the stimulus of this strenuous competition and that of the even earlier London Power Omnibus Company on the Edgware Road (also an exponent of the fleetname, in this case *Pioneer*) horse bus operators had little choice but to embark upon motorisation. The London General Omnibus Co Ltd, largest of them by far, ordered Swiss Orion chassis and French De Dion, and the London Road Car Co Ltd, user of a trademark in the form of the Union Flag, ordered German Büssing chassis from Sydney Straker & Squire of Bristol and displayed the fleetname *Union Jack*. At the end of 1905 Road Car made history by operating a Putney—Mile End Station service right across the City—the first regular mechanically-propelled service in the City since Hancock's day, 70 years previously.

The preponderance of foreign makes in the early days is not surprising when the way British manufacturers had been denied a home market owing to repressive legislation is taken into account. True, Pioneer used Scott-Stirling petrol-engined vehicles and there were some Clarkson steamers, built at Chelmsford, in the early motor fleets, including in 1904 the first General motor to carry fare-paying passengers, but for a year or two London was a happy hunting ground for Continental salesmen. The Belgian Germaine, the French Turgan, Lacoste & Battman, Brillie and Ducommun, the German Scheibler, and Dürkopp were other makes which appeared before 1907 was out; they were accompanied by two other vehicles of French origin—the battery-powered Electromobile and the steam Darracq-Serpollet, which lasted longer than their petrol rivals—the electrics revived by "Dr" Brighton until replaced in wartime by Tilling-Stevens petrol-electrics and the steam buses of a second generation in London until the autumn of 1912.

By 1905 a thin trickle of British designed and built buses was appearing—the steam enthusiasts at Leyland had given way so far as using Crossley petrol engines, Clarkson at Chelmsford had put a man-sized steam generator under a driver perched high in the air, like the coachmen of the steam drays of the 1830s, and Dennis was marketing a very modern petrol-engined chassis with worm drive. Straker-Squires not merely cribbed from Büssing designs were available, with Maudslay, Thornycroft and the Scottish Arrol-Johnston from 1906 and in the following year the Ryknield, Armstrong-Whitworth and Wolseley (a highly successful type) came on the streets.

Whatever their origin these vehicles combined to provide a pretty poor bunch. One of my earliest bus memories is of sitting on an open-top De Dion which had come to a dead stand on the north side of Hyde Park—just as it had begun to rain, it goes without saying—and the receding prospects of ever seeing the promised Franco-British exhibition at the White City. Another is of a bus which actually failed by a few yards to reach Bow police station where a proportion of the hackney carriage licensing was done and the chagrin of the driver as he arranged for it to be towed back to the Old Kent Road garage which Vanguard had acquired from the London County Council tramways. I have since learned of the perambulating mechanics employed by Vanguard whose duties were to repair broken down buses on the street, get the failure going and then ride on the service until they spotted the next driver in trouble with his recalcitrant steed.

So the early motor bus business in London had achieved several things—mostly unintentional. It had ruined the horse bus business; it had made the new tube railways, geared as they were to compete with the horse bus, less remunerative than their capital-intensive structure required; and by low fares and high repair costs it had ruined itself. As it always does, unrestrained competition in passenger transport was leading to disaster.

The first step towards combating incipient bankruptcy was taken by Sir George Gibb, deputy chairman of the Underground Electric Railways Company of London, who brought together all the parties concerned in a London Passenger Traffic Conference, held on July 22, 1907. The result was an agreement on fares by the end of the year and more lasting results from friendships formed during the negotiations. This took the form of a merger of the London General Omnibus Company, the Vanguard Motor Omnibus Company and the London Road Car Company, arranged as from July 1, 1908. The enlarged LGOC possessed a fleet of over 900 motor vehicles, although not all of them were runners; it acquired a good deal of know-how from its constituents, including the service number idea introduced by George Samuel Dicks on Vanguard routes. Services 1 and 2 today still bear a resemblance to routes inaugurated by Vanguard from Brondesbury to the Law Courts (and later to Waterloo) and along the Finchley Road, nearly 70 years ago.

The second part of the recovery process was to try to get the mechanical engineering right. When Frank Searle joined the General in 1907 he found chaotic conditions, with up to 28 different types in one garage, among which were a high proportion of casualties owing to lack of spares. He made quick recommendations for segregation of makes into garages and rationalisation of spares and found himself chief engineer after three months service. The enterprising Vanguard group had a factory at Walthamstow under the care of the Motor Omnibus Construction Co Ltd and this was to play a great part in his plans.

These were accelerated by the new and stringent regulations covering construction and use of motor buses which were issued by Sir Edward Henry, Commissioner of Metropolitan Police, on August 30, 1909. These cribbed, cabined and confined the motor bus as never before. A maximum of 34 seats, 18 up and 16 down, was laid down; the length was limited to 23ft including the rear platform, and the maximum width to 7ft 2in; bodywork dimensions were specified in great detail, as were destination and route boards. The last-mentioned had to read geographically in accordance with the direction of travel. But biggest blow to operators or manufacturers was the limitation of unladen weight to $3\frac{1}{2}$ tons or a total laden weight of 6 tons, counting the 34 passengers and the driver and conductor at 140 lb each.

Protests were made at once that this would kill the motor bus stone dead by reducing the only possible sort of vehicle to a 16-seat single-decker which could not hope to earn its living. This may have been the intention, for the motor bus had gathered many enemies, among them Aubrey Llewellyn Coventry Fell, chief officer of the London County Council Tramways, who, although a pioneer user of motor lorries for permanent way work, saw this as a means of vanquishing a commercial rival and gave it as his opinion that the motor bus would not exist outside museums in ten years' time. That was in September, 1909; but the intention of Scotland Yard to limit weights had been well-known and in the preceding month the LGOC works at Walthamstow had completed the first of its lightweight silent motor buses, the X type. Very quickly Leyland and Straker-Squire produced models to meet the London regulations and Clarkson produced a steamer which filled the bill for the National fleet. There was also a new lightweight Darracq-Serpollet steam bus from France, but built in London. This lighter bus movement was helped by a rapid technological advance including steel wheels in place of the clumsy wooden artillery wheels which needed costly attention in hot weather by soaking in vats of water after the day's work.

It was Frank Searle who had the brainwave of constructing a bus to meet LGOC requirements when the company had been about to order more Wolseleys or De Dions as their most reliable types. His first cast, the X, used reliable components out of a wide range of makes, and was referred to in snide descriptions as a "Daimler-Wolseley-Straker." The prototype took until December to get approval from the police and then 60 others were put in hand; the police tussles, mainly over noise, produced some new ideas and with the aid of Walter James Iden as works manager, plans were made for designing something better and producing it in quantity. The big mistake with the X type turned out to be a rather literal compliance with the regulation that said speed must not exceed 12 mph at its highest, or alternatively that if 12 mph was exceeded there should be an audible warning.

They were distinctly sluggish and were all confined to Service 7, Liverpool Street & Wormwood Scrubs, in later years.

The new model was completed and licensed in October, 1910, and by the end of 1911 nearly 500 B-type had appeared. It not only complied with regulations, it was extraordinarily reliable and at last gave promise of viability to the harassed motor bus industry, so that the LGOC staked a lot of money on a production scheme that worked up to 30 vehicles a week in 1912. Broken-down and police-stopped buses disappeared; the long lines of thirsty vehicles queuing at Aldgate pump for radiator water vanished and a good many of the rival fleet liveries vanished with them, unable to stand the losses on motor bus operation. But the existence of new lightweight buses from the chassis builders, which held out promise of cheaper operation, attracted some new capital to have a go at the goldmine of the capital's streets. Sometimes investors were a bit niggardly; Metropolitan Steam Omnibus Co Ltd, using Darracq-Serpollets, seems to have built only 43 of the intended 100; Clarkson gradually pushed his white National fleet of steamers, built at Chelmsford, to 173, by 1914. Benjamin Richardson, of the London & Suburban Company, operated routes from Kingston and from a garage at Walworth (an old horse tram depot), on Kingsway, the latest new Central London street. With Leyland investment the company became the London Central, and then with big ideas of a fleet of 650, the New Central, which based its prospectus on the agreement it inherited with the General to run 35 vehicles on Kingsway without LGOC competition. Investors did not agree and the issue was a flop.

In the meantime the Great Eastern of London, derived from the horse-bus subsidiary of an unsuccessful eastern suburban tramway, had been snatching customers from the local municipal tramways and giving the General a run for its money between Leyton and Ilford and the West End and West Kilburn, with garages at Leyton, Forest Gate and West Kilburn. It ordered 100 chain-driven Straker-Squires to replace its massive

Top to bottom: A white Clarkson steamer on the National summer Sunday service from Peckham Rye to Petersham; the last of the Great Eastern chain-driven Straker-Squires was delivered in the summer of 1911 in General all-red livery as Y52; from October 1912 the Metropolitan Steam Omnibus fleet was replaced by LGOC B-type petrol buses.

Arrol-Johnstons and ageing Straker-Squires of Büssing derivation. It had flirted with Union Jack on mergers and pooling and then had conversations with the new General management, keenly pointed by cut-throat competition which led to actual collisions between rival buses. As the lovely egg-yellow Strakers appeared, glorious with flossy blue-rimmed gilt lettered fleet-names on a red background on the side panels, negotiations on price proceeded, but in April "Generalisation" of the route boards began and service numbers, 35, 36, 37, were allotted to Great Eastern workings. The last bus was licensed to Great Eastern on May 24, 1911, and the remainder of the order, up to number 52, appeared in General crimson, with bonnet numbers in a "Y" series. Straker-Squire resolved not to be excluded from the London market for ever; they had a small order from W. P. Allen in 1913, but their resentment at the cancellation of the 48 Great Easterns boiled up eventually in endeavours in 1922 to found an "ex-servicemen's bus company", wildly anticipating a 3000-strong fleet of SS buses.

The sudden financial resurgence of the General, its excellent home-built bus, the demise of the horse bus (which had been running in greater numbers than motors in London until they equalised on October 31, 1910) and the proliferation of General B types, mainly responsible for raising the London motor fleet from 1149 to 1641 during 1912, caused the British Electric Traction group to have fears for its Metropolitan Electric Tramways. The American-financed Underground Electric Railways of London feared for their precariously profitable tube system. It began during 1911 to buy LGOC shares and eventually took it over in March, 1912, "as from January 1". The General's expansion plans of new garages and more buses continued and the new owners formed a new LGOC with wider powers, including ability to run 30 instead of 15 miles from Charing Cross. Co-ordinated services from Underground stations were begun, the first being from Hounslow Barracks (now Hounslow West) station on July 14, 1912, and linking the District Railway with Harlington, Staines, and more spectacularly, with Windsor, on which the tentatively suggested hourly service had to be made 12 buses an hour on Sundays to clear the queues. Short feeder services began from outposts of the Underground—Ealing Broadway, Putney Bridge, Finsbury Park and Barking among others—rather like the new route pattern that accompanied one-man and flat fare innovations of recent years.

The Underground-backed LGOC made a new agreement in May, 1912, with Thos. Tilling, Ltd, for the latter to operate 150 of their petrol-electric buses (evolved in 1911) in conjunction with the LGOC. This was a reward for having helped fend off competition from Daimler-built KPL (Knight-Pieper-Lanchester) petrol-electrics with twin motors instead of a differential; these were alleged to infringe Tilling-Stevens patents. Daimler had been interested in the Pieper Automixte system since 1906 and built a clumsy prototype for the Gearless Motor Omnibus Co Ltd. After the KPL blow, Daimler decided to produce a bus very similar to the B-type with a Knight sleeve-valve engine driving through a gearbox. Searle, who had left the General in 1911 for Daimler, managed an order for 350 buses from the BET for Tramways (MET) but he was no match for the chief executive of the Underground group, Albert Stanley, who later became Lord Ashfield. At the end of 1912 the BET agreed that the MET buses should operate under LGOC direction and that only 226 of them should be Daimlers; it was also agreed that the 33 Daimlers which British Automobile Traction had ordered from Daimler for London service should in future work LGOC services instead of the freelancing they were so far doing, mainly between Liverpool Street Station and Victoria. Incidentally they operated from a garage in Camden Town which had housed the motor buses of Associated Omnibus Co Ltd, a horse bus operator who had motorised disastrously in the latter part of 1905, and sold its 29 motor buses after withdrawing them in July, 1907; the Great Western Railway was the largest purchaser. Daimler had

129

other orders for BET companies in compensation for the cut in the MET order and at last its Gearless Omnibus Co Ltd got a foothold on the London streets, with 20 buses to work as directed by the General—but Daimlers with mechanical and not petrol-electric transmission. Daimler lost the MET maintenance contract and instead became sales outlet for the LGOC B-type bus and lorry chassis built in the works at Walthamstow, which by now had been transferred to an Underground subsidiary, the Associated Equipment Co Ltd.

These Daimler fleets emerged from the autumn of 1912 onwards till the late summer of 1913; the green British came first on October 7, 1912, and worked with the LGOC under agreement of January 22, 1913. A few days later the blue MET fleet began to operate from the Colindale and Tottenham garages originally intended as bases for extension of the tramways influence to Watford and St Albans outward and into the central area inward. The Gearless fleet was in a silver-grey livery at first when it appeared in April but later the MET blue was used. The 124 remaining MET buses appeared on AEC B-type chassis in blue livery with the registration numbers reserved for the Daimlers in the first place. Knowing nothing of the struggles between the British Electric Traction and Underground groups it was a very exciting morning for me when a blue Daimler, with shining new varnished route boards on a new service, 51, from West Kilburn to Ilford, overtook me on the way to school.

The first time AEC B-type buses had been allotted to another London operator was in the autumn of 1912. The unfortunate Associated company already mentioned had operated horse buses until that year, when it still possessed 106, with over 1100 horses. It had taken over several LGOC horse services when that company gave them up on October 25, 1911, and now it proposed to re-motorise with 50 Daimlers. This persuaded the LGOC to offer terms for providing and running and maintaining (at 8½d a mile) 55 B-types which Associated bought for £50,000 at a time when they cost about £350 each complete.

In General crimson with Associated in even capitals along the side panel the buses were operated on five routes from four garages, 10 to each route with one spare. The first began from London Bridge to Muswell Hill on 43 on October 4, 1912 and I had the good fortune to see the new operator (or 'co-operator') as one crossed the path of a 25 I was riding on at the Bank of England.

Another agreement of October 16, 1912, brought a fleet of 100 B-type on the road in the livery of the Metropolitan Steam Omnibus Co Ltd, green with the fleet-name on a dove-grey panel surmounting a crest. That concern's Darracq-Serpollets had been run off the road by competing Generals in the earlier part of the year. One of the steamers survived in the Isle of Wight until 1923. The Metropolitan Steam buses were all at Willesden Garage, whereas MET were housed at Hendon, Tottenham, Putney, Streatham and Plumstead, and Associated at Holloway, Palmers Green, Albany Street and Shepherds Bush.

From January, 1913, the New Central Omnibus Company vehicles were running in conjunction with the General from Penrose Street, Walworth and Kingston garages. These Leylands had a basically pale yellow livery with "Central" in gold letters on a dark blue or black ground with some red lining. Later in the year the Southern buses appeared —10 Bs in blue livery and owned by the South Metropolitan Electric Tramways & Lighting Co Ltd—result of the late signing of yet another agreement derived from the BET-General dialogues of 1912 which had as an incidental outcome the solemn promise of the LGOC not to compete with Greenock & Port Glasgow Tramways Company and the Airdrie & Coatbridge Tramways Company, both signed on November 19, 1912, nearly a month before the signatures were placed to the one that mattered, that with Tramways (MET) Omnibus Co Ltd.

The summer of 1913 brought another delight—as they emerged from their annual overhaul some General buses assumed a red/white/green livery, the last-mentioned a sort of rich eau-de-nil mainly on the rocker

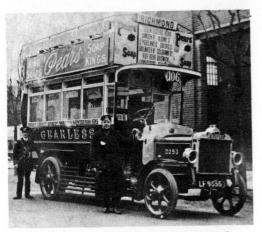

The Gearless fleet of 22 Daimlers came on to the London streets during 1913 "to work as directed" by the LGOC. The livery was at first silver grey, but this view depicts one on the Sunday and holiday route from Tottenham to Richmond, which ceased in January 1914, in blue.

The Tramways (MET) fleet was intended to consist of 350 CC-type Daimlers, of which only 226 were delivered. The last 124 vehicles were LGOC B-type buses in dark blue and the whole fleet worked under General direction.

panel and stairs; though it was short-lived, I thought it was the most attractive colour scheme on the London streets.

The National Steam Car Co Ltd, which had been operating an increasing fleet of Clarksons since 1909 from garages at Putney Bridge and Nunhead, was now persuaded to join the establishment and from January 1, 1914, its fleet of white naphtha-burning steamers operated on services numbered in the General list and after a comparatively short time mostly on services established by the LGOC.

The last competitors to be set up came in 1913—William Percy Allen with some primrose shaft-driven Straker-Squires and Premier Omnibus Co Ltd, a company of complicated origins which produced six red overtype De Dions on the favourite Liverpool Street-Victoria run. As the Allen Omnibus Co Ltd and London Premier they operated together between the City and West Kilburn and ran into hard times during the latter part of 1916. A receiver for Allen and winding up for Premier resulted and for a few weeks, until petrol restrictions due to the War killed them, there were two LGOC replacement services.

The standardisation of livery to the

General's then current vermilion/broken white began in 1914. The New Central assets were bought by the Underground Electric group in October 1913 and they were sold to the LGOC as from June 30, 1914; thereafter the Central's distinctive livery disappeared. With the outbreak of war the MET and Gearless Daimlers were sold back and eventually went to war service; some of the B replacements appeared in red with MET as fleetname, but because the Metropolitan Steam company was taken over by the LGOC at the end of 1914, the fleet name Metropolitan became available and was used on MET vehicles from some time in 1915. Gearless and Southern vehicles also appeared in red; the Tilling London fleet had been dark red since the first TTA1 petrol-electric of 1911 which reputedly made its first appearance in green. The National fleet of white-painted steamers was withdrawn in November, 1919 (rocketing price of fuel and labour, plus the hostility of the Metropolitan Police who lined up flash boilers with gelignite) after which red uniformity and dull, sensible overall co-ordination with financial stability prevailed until Arthur George Partridge and his friends opened up with his Chocolate Express Leyland in 1922. But that is another story.

131

Acknowledgements

I am happy to be able to thank the writers
and photographers who responded to my
requests for articles and photo-features for
Buses Annual 1973.

The photographs in photo-features are
credited on the respective pages. The other
photos are by

AEC: 105.
John Aldridge: 73, 80 (bottom), 90 (lower), 91.
Berliet: 79 (centre).
Gavin Booth: Cover, 67 (bottom left),
   79 (bottom).
D. G. Bowen: 35, 36 (centre).
Stewart J. Brown: 21–29.
Bussing: 75, 77 (top).
G. Coxon: 110.
DAF: 72, 79 (top).
Daimler-Benz: 78 (top).
T. Davies: 103.
J. E. Dunabin: 107, 108.
Fiat: 80 (top).
R. A. Golds: 81–83.
Robert E. Jowitt: 56–64.
Charles Klapper Collection: 124, 128 (top), 128
   (bottom).
London Transport: 86, 90 (upper).
MAN: 77 (centre).
Magirus-Deutz: 77 (bottom).
Gavin Martin: 87, 89, 95.
W. G. Morris: 101.
A. Moyes: 113–120.
T. W. Moore: 2/3.
George Robbins Collection: 125, 128 (centre), 131.
Park Royal: 84/85, 94.
John Parke: 37–44, 104, 106.
Scania: 74, 80 (centre).
Setra: 78 (centre).
Thornycroft: 7, 9, 10, 13, 15.
W. M. Thomas: 100.
G. H. Truran: 36 (top, bottom).
Van Hool: 78 (foot).
R. L. Wilson: 109, 111, 112.

In addition, I am grateful to Travel Press and
the National Bus Company for lending the
colour plates on pages 65–68.